A CELEBRATION

OF CHRISTMAS

A CELEBRATION

OF CHRISTMAS

A COLLECTION OF STORIES, POEMS, ESSAYS
AND TRADITIONS BY FAVORITE LDS AUTHORS

Deseret Book Company
Salt Lake City, Utah

No part of this book may be reproduced in any
form or by any means without permission in writing
from the publisher, Deseret Book Company,
P.O. Box 30178, Salt Lake City, Utah 84130.
Deseret Book is a registered trademark of
Deseret Book Company.

First printing September 1988

Library of Congress Cataloging-in-Publication Data

A Celebration of Christmas.
    Includes index.
    1. Christmas—United States.   2. Mormons—United
States—Social life and customs.
GT4986.A1C38   1988   394.2′68282′0973   88-20337
ISBN 0-87579-176-X

CONTENTS

GIFTS OF SELF
  Ardeth Kapp 1

THE TRUE SPIRIT OF CHRISTMAS
  S. Michael Wilcox 4

AWAY IN A MANGER
  Lael Littke 10

A CHRISTMAS SONG
  Jack Weyland 17

MAYBE CHRISTMAS DOESN'T COME
FROM A STORE
  Jeffrey R. Holland 25

REFLECTIONS ON THE CHRISTMAS STORY
  Gerald N. Lund 30

CHRISTMAS EVE IN FRONT OF
THE OPEN OVEN DOOR
  Leonard J. Arrington 41

AARON'S CHRISTMAS TREE
  Alma J. Yates 45

THE JOY OF CHRISTMAS
  Dell Van Orden 50

THE OLD WREATH
  Lowell M. Durham, Jr. 52

Contents

THE SIFTING
Lowell M. Durham, Jr. 53

THE NIGHT AFTER CHRISTMAS
Kris Mackay. 54

A CHRISTMAS NEEDLEPOINT
Brent A. Barlow. 57

THE MEANING OF CHRISTMAS
Lowell L. Bennion 62

A PICTURE-PERFECT CHRISTMAS
Janene Wolsey Baadsgaard 65

MOM WAS REALLY SANTA CLAUS
Dennis L. Lythgoe 67

CHRISTMAS SNOWS, CHRISTMAS WINDS
Don Marshall 70

THE CHRISTMAS LETTER
Karla Erickson 77

ANTICIPATION OF THE SHEPHERDS
Richard Tice 79

ALL THE PROPHETS
Richard Tice 80

THIS OLD BIBLE
Richard Tice and Jack Lyon 81

CHRISTMAS AWAY FROM HOME
Mary Ellen Edmunds 82

CREATIVE HOLIDAY IDEAS
Dian Thomas 85

I KNOW WHO SANTA CLAUS IS
Carroll Hofeling Morris 88

GENTLE JESUS
Mabel Jones Gabbott 96

WHEN LOVE CAME DOWN
   Mabel Jones Gabbott   97

CHRISTMAS BREADS
   Dora D. Flack   98

THE SQUASH-BLOSSOM NECKLACE
   Blaine M. and Brenton G. Yorgason   102

A CELEBRATION OF CHRISTMAS
   Marilynne and Richard Linford   109

FAVORITE HOLIDAY FARE
   Winnifred C. Jardine   118

HOLIDAY RECIPES
   Helen Thackeray   120

BECAUSE OF ONE SMALL CHILD
   Mabel Jones Gabbott   123

FOR ALL MANKIND
   Mabel Jones Gabbott   124

SURPRISE ME FOR CHRISTMAS
   Shirley Sealy   126

THE CHRISTMAS WHEN THE WIND
DID NOT BLOW
   Jaroldeen Edwards   129

PRICELESS GIFTS
   Daryl V. Hoole   138

WARM HANDS FOR CHRISTMAS
   Marilynne Todd Linford   140

GIFTS OF SELF

by Ardeth G. Kapp

It was Christmas Eve. The magic of Christmas seemed more real this year, not so much from the lights and tinsel but the feeling of excitement from the inside out. Family members had gathered at our house. After our traditional family dinner, Grandpa gathered us in the living room where he opened the Bible and read once again the Christmas story from Luke.

"And it came to pass in those days, that there went out a decree from Caesar Augustus" (Luke 2:1), and the story continued. I noticed his hands trembling as he held the sacred record. Grandpa's voice was weaker now, but strong in the message that he and Grandma knew in their hearts and had taught us through the years. After the stockings were finally hung and treats left for Santa, the children reluctantly, yet eagerly, doubled up in beds trying hard to get to sleep while listening intensely for any sounds from the expected night visitor. Finally, one by one, each family member had slipped off to bed. The fire was burning low. Now if my husband, Heber, would just go to bed, I could finish my gift for

him. I needed about three more hours to complete the plan I had been so excited about and working on for months. But in spite of my encouragement for him to leave, he lingered. It was evident he would wait for me. I decided to go to bed and wait until he dropped off to sleep, then slip out and finish my project for him.

With the lights out and the house quiet, I lay in bed looking into the dark. I was too excited to sleep. I waited to hear his heavy breathing announcing that it would be safe to slip away. To my amazement, and after only a little time, he whispered, "Ardie." I didn't respond. A conversation now would only delay the time before I could finish my work. When I didn't answer, he slipped out of bed as cautiously as I had planned to. What was he up to? I would go to sleep, I decided. If I could sleep now and awaken about 3:00 A.M. I could still finish my project before six o'clock in the morning, the time Grandpa Ted had agreed we should all gather around the tree.

I woke up off and on during the short night, glanced at the lighted clock, saw that Heber was still not in bed, and tried again to doze off. But I didn't want to fall too soundly asleep and spoil the plan I had been working on so diligently.

Finally, I again woke up, and this time I realized Heber was getting into bed ever so quietly. It was only minutes until his heavy breathing assured me that he was sound asleep. It was 3:00 A.M. If all went well, in three hours I could still complete this special gift on time. I knew he would be pleased. "But what in the world kept him up half the night?" I wondered. In just a few hours, I would know; but for now I must concentrate and work fast.

Months ago we had talked about the forthcoming Christmas and made the traditional gift list that ranged from the ridiculous to the sublime. At the top of my list was a wish that we could have more time together for him to teach me of his great understanding of the gospel. But I was driving two hours each day to BYU, and his schedule was very busy. Our time together was precious.

Heber's list of wants was short, as usual; but he did express a concern for the responsibility he had as a stake president to lead the way, and it bothered him that his family history was not compiled. His family group sheets were incomplete. While the information was probably available from aunts and uncles, his own brothers and sisters had little or no information. He felt anxious about this, but wasn't sure it was a Christmas list item, at least not the kind you could get from the mail-order catalog or even ZCMI. That was months ago, and now my prayer was being answered. The hands on my watch seemed to stand still while I worked. Everything was coming together so beautifully.

The gift was finally wrapped. I could hardly believe I had done it, but there it was—the evidence of hours and hours of work. I hurried back and slipped into bed. It was 5:45 A.M. I had made it! It didn't matter now, and it's a good thing, because children's voices were heard from the other room. "Grandpa says it's time we can get up. Hurry, hurry. We can't wait," they said. And neither could I. There were so many gifts for everyone.

Heber handed me a package. What in the world could it be? I opened it. It was a box of cassette tapes. On the top of the box was a message, "My dear Ardie. While you are traveling each day, I will be with you and will teach you. As you know, the Doctrine and Covenants has been of special interest to me over the years. I have enjoyed reading and recording for you the entire book. Reading it with the purpose of sharing it with you, I have endeavored to express my interpretation and feelings so that you might feel what I feel about this sacred book. I finished it only a few hours ago. It has been a most rewarding experience for me. Remember the Lord's promise, 'Therefore, if you will ask of me you shall receive; if you will knock it shall be opened unto you. Now, as you have asked, behold, I say unto you, keep my commandments, and seek to bring forth and establish the cause of Zion; Seek not for riches but for wisdom, and behold, the mysteries of God shall be unfolded unto you, and then shall you be made rich. Behold, he that hath eternal life is rich.' (D&C 6:5-7.) May these tapes add to your wisdom and help unfold the mysteries of God and prepare us for our eternal life together.''

I immediately thought of my friend who had recently lost her husband with cancer and wondered what price she would pay for such a gift, to be able to hear her husband's voice read the scriptures to her and her children over and over again, even in his absence. What a priceless gift! No wonder some of his meetings had seemed to last longer than usual. How could I ever thank him enough?

I handed Heber my gift. He tore off the cover. A book. A book of remembrance—full. Pages and pages with pictures and stories never before recorded, a result of many secret trips to Ogden while he was in his many meetings, interviewing relatives and sorting through records and histories. The first page of

the gift began with a letter, ''Dear Heber. As I have copied, reviewed, and prepared these sheets and interviewed family members, your ancestors have become very real to me, and I have an increased appreciation and understanding of the greatness and nobility in the man I married. In interviews with those who knew and remembered your parents, I learned that your father always wanted your mother to be with him, in the fields if possible, and even wherever he was in the house. You must have inherited that. Although I never met your father, and your mother only once, when we meet, I know I'll love them and know them better because of this gift I have prepared for you, which really has been a gift for me.''

I don't remember any of the other gifts that year, but Heber and I will never forget the spirit of that glorious Christmas celebration.

Ardeth G. Kapp, general president of the Young Women, has a number of books to her credit, including I Walk By Faith, Miracles in Pinafores and Bluejeans, The Gentle Touch, *and* Echoes from My Prairie. *This article was first published in the* Church News, *December 1986.*

THE TRUE SPIRIT OF CHRISTMAS

by S. Michael Wilcox

When I was a little boy, people told me that the true spirit of Christmas was the spirit of giving; but I didn't believe them. I knew that the true spirit of Christmas was getting. I could hardly wait until Christmas morning when my mother would stand at the door to the living room that separated me from a wonder of toys. She would peek through and tell me Santa had been here and express her surprise that he had given me so much. Then I was obliged to eat breakfast, make my bed, brush my teeth, and get dressed. The anxiety and anticipation this caused is impossible to describe. By the time I attacked the neatly wrapped packages and saw the delights they contained, I was filled with a joy and relief I have not found comparable to any joy on earth.

I remember the year I grew up. That was the year Christmas lost its magic and I began to say, like the adults around me, "The true spirit of Christmas is giving." I found there *was* satisfaction in giving. But the magic never returned, and each year as the tree was decorated and the lights were hung on the front porch I wondered if Christmas wasn't a whole lot better when I thought more about what I received and less about what I gave.

The years went on and I became a man, giving to my children and secretly envying their sheer delight at receiving the marvelous gifts of Christmas.

A few years ago I read very carefully the story of the first Christmas in the Americas. To my wonder and delight I discovered I had been right as a child—the true spirit of Christmas *was* the spirit of receiving. Since then, the wonder of Christmas has returned.

Let me take you in your imagination back to Zarahemla in the year 5 B.C. and let us live together the most marvelous Christmas story ever written.

The year 5 B.C. is an interesting and challenging time to be a Christian. Our generation is an unstable one. We have seen the people shift from wickedness to righteousness and back to wickedness again. We have seen the slow erosion of our laws until Nephi II, our great prophet and chief judge, gives up the seat of government, weary with his inability to cause positive reform. He decides the only way to reform and save his people is in "bearing down in pure testimony," as his ancestor Alma had done.

We have seen the rise of the Gadianton robbers. They have filled the judgment seats. They have assassinated their opponents, and they wield great power. About ten years ago we saw Nephi bring the people to their knees in repentance through a prolonged famine that ended for a time the self-destructive wars of our people. But the people quickly forgot the lesson and have been slipping ever so quickly back into their materialistic and proud ways.

Most marvelous of all, we have witnessed the end of an era of interracial wars between the Nephites and Lamanites. As youth, roughly twenty-five years ago, we witnessed the conversion of the entire Lamanite nation through the preaching of Nephi and his brother Lehi.

We are adults now with families. Nephi is older, though still actively leading the Church and preaching the gospel. But there are dark clouds on the horizon. The strength of the Gadianton robbers is growing again, and the intensity of faith seems to be waning in the Church. As prosperity flourishes, the lessons of the past are forgotten. It is an interesting and challenging time to live.

Recently there has been a Lamanite prophet named Samuel preaching in the streets and markets of Zarahemla. Though we don't know it, he is about to test our faith and the faith of all the Christians in the land.

The Nephites, unwilling to listen to the exhortations of Samuel, have cast him out; but as we enter the city, we notice a large crowd in a state of great excitement gathered near the walls. There on the wall stands Samuel. He has returned. His message has not changed from his earlier warnings.

An acquaintance of ours approaches us as we listen. He is one who has relinquished his faith and is caught up in the materialistic greed of a Gadianton society.

"What do you think of this Lamanite?" he asks us.

"He is a prophet," we answer.

"So he proclaims. Then you believe in his predictions?"

"We accept all the words of a prophet."

As we listen, Samuel begins to speak of Christ, predicting his birth after five years pass. This is not a new or strange prophecy, for Lehi predicted the Savior would be born six hundred years after he left Jerusalem. Those with faith and a calendar know He will come in five years, but our acquaintance asks us, "Do you believe this, that Christ will come after five years?"

"Yes," we reply. "It has been prophesied from the very beginning by many prophets." Our acquaintance comments with a mocking tone about the "convenience" of having Christ born across the sea, in another land, making true verification impossible. And had Samuel not continued under the inspiration of the Lord, our faith would not be tried; but Samuel continued.

"And behold, this will I give unto you for a sign at the time of his coming; for behold, there shall be great lights in heaven, insomuch that in the night before he cometh there shall be no darkness, insomuch that it shall appear unto man as if it was day.

"Therefore, there shall be one day and a night and a day, as if it were one day and there were no night; and this shall be unto you for a sign; for ye shall know of the rising of the sun and also of its setting; therefore they shall know of a surety that there shall be two days and a night; nevertheless the night shall not be darkened; and it shall be the night before he is born.

"And behold, there shall a new star arise, such an one as ye never have beheld; and this also shall be a sign unto you."

Let us pause a moment in our narrative. I have often wondered how I would have accepted that pronouncement. I am sure I would have looked at the sun with a certain uneasiness. I am sure I would have watched it set that night and felt with a growing fear the darkness settle over the land. I cannot think of a single prophetic utterance in all of scripture so completely remarkable as this one. What boldness and courage it took to utter it! What faith and courage it took to receive it!

As we try to comprehend the impact of this prophecy, our acquaintance, with a certain delight, turns and asks, "You certainly don't believe that, do you?"

We hesitate. If only Nephi II had uttered it, not a Lamanite prophet newly arrived in Zarahemla. Our acquaintance notices our hesitation.

"Because of course," he continues, "it is absolutely and utterly impossible for the sun to go down and it remain as light as day. You know that, don't you?"

I would like to believe that I would have had the faith and the whispered assurances of the Spirit so that I could have answered the critics and the mockers. I would have wanted to say, "Yes, I believe Samuel has spoken under the direction of the Holy Ghost and that this sign will come."

Perhaps our skeptical friend would have answered, "Then you're a bigger fool than I imagined. But for your sake I hope it comes."

There is the hint of a veiled threat in his words that we do not yet comprehend. We listen with uneasiness to the rest of Samuel's message, but the words "one day and a night and a day" haunt our thoughts. The crowd becomes more and more agitated. Suddenly they are shooting arrows and slinging stones at the figure on the wall; but they cannot hit him, and the words of Samuel continue. When they approach to bind him, his message delivered, Samuel leaps from the wall to return to his own people. "He was never heard of more among the Nephites."

What reflection is contained in that single last line in Helaman! In the coming months and years, how often would we have wanted to hear Samuel assure us that his words were inspired, that he knew the sign would come, that he was sure of God's promise and the coming of the Christ child? But he would not be seen among the Nephites again.

How often would our scorning friends pick at our faith, during those months and years, seeking to enlarge the tiny doubts we try to keep from entering our minds.

"Where is your Lamanite prophet?" they would ask us. "Why do you suppose he's never returned? He didn't stay to see the sun set, night after night, did he? But I imagine even a Lamanite prophet knows when he has uttered foolishness. Give up this ridiculous belief. It will always be dark when the sun sets. How can it be otherwise?"

The Lord knows how to test his people. There is, however, one thing that we would have had on our side—Nephi. He is still the prophet, and he assures the faithful "of things which must shortly come." The Nephi to whom God gave all power is with us. The Nephi who humbled these same people with famine leads us. The Nephi who stood face to face with the corrupt lawyers and Gadianton robbers, predicting their assassinations, revealing their evil plans, and bearing witness of their sins, stands at our head. With Nephi our fears are calmed; but every night we watch the sun set, and every night the darkness returns.

When would the fears and doubts,

the straining for faith, have become almost unbearable? The first year? The second? The third? What would have been our thoughts as the opposition grew and their mocking became increasingly threatening? How strong would our faith have been when the fifth year began and the sun set and the night came? How would our fears have increased when the power of the unbelievers became great, and they proclaimed a day on which all the believers who did not renounce their faith would be put to death if the sign didn't come? I wonder how I would have felt as I watched the twilight deepen night after night and thought of my children sleeping and the fate that awaited them if the night grew dark one time too many.

More and more we would have turned to Nephi to hear his calm assurance of faith—"The sign will come, the sign will come." But there would have been other voices; and though we would have tried to shut them out, at night in the stillness they would have come and repeated the question asked so often, "How can there be light when there is no sun?"

Sometime during that last year a new factor enters the test. Nephi II, the strength of our people, is taken by the Lord. He gives his son Nephi III charge concerning the plates and "departs out of the land, and whither he went no man knoweth."

How would this knowledge have greeted us? What doubts would it have sparked anew? If Nephi II had died, we could have mourned his loss; but there would have been no awakened opportunity for doubt. But when he just disappears, it is hard to deny new suspicions.

"Where is your great prophet Nephi?" the unbelievers might have challenged. "Has he abandoned you to your deaths as Samuel did? Why do you think he left the way he did, sneaking into the wilderness to save his own life? Even he knows the sign is an impossibility. Are you still so stubborn in your old traditions that you can't face reality? There will be no Christ!"

On and on the mocking and challenging continue, and as we eagerly wait for the sunset each evening the smiles of silent reproach widen on the faces of those who anticipate the appointed day of destruction.

How would we have felt those last weeks as we "watched steadfastly for that night and that day"? Would not our prayers have been fervent and deep and full of meaning? How does it feel to have hope dashed with every setting sun?

How would we have felt the last days while our enemies prepared themselves for the coming slaughter? On the last day Nephi, with deep concern, kneels and cries "mightily" for his people. The Lord speaks peace to him saying, "On this night shall the sign be given." But Nephi cannot spread those words of comfort in a single day. The people's faith will be tested to the last rays of the setting sun.

The scriptures are not clear on the method of destruction planned for the believers. Perhaps they were rounded up into the center of their cities or outside the walls where at sunset they would be put to the sword. Perhaps mob rule prevailed and every man sought out his neighbors. As believers, with our families we watch from our homes the setting sun. If given a final chance that afternoon to save our lives by renouncing our belief in the Savior, would we have done so? Would we have thought that if the sign didn't come, life would have no meaning, for a life without Christ is no life at all?

Holding the hands of our families we step into the open light of late afternoon and watch what may be our last sunset. There is that moment when the sun hangs trembling at the brink of the horizon. It slips out of sight. There is a moment of hesitation, watching, hoping, and questioning. "Is it getting dark? Are our lives forfeit?" Then there is that moment when the realization enters our hearts that the darkness is not gathering. It is getting, on the contrary, lighter and lighter.

If we can picture that moment, if we can transport ourselves past barriers of time, place, and culture, we will hear a sound. It is the sound of Christmas. It is the sound of weeping, the sound of gratitude, the sound of joy and triumph and faith renewed and vindicated. It is the sound of mankind receiving with a love beyond words the incomparable gift of the Son of God into the world. It is the true spirit of Christmas—which isn't the spirit of giving at all, but the spirit of receiving, receiving the love of our Father and His Son, and in its reception with thankfulness giving God the only gift He seeks, that of a broken heart and contrite spirit. What a moment and what a sound that is! May its sound ring through all our Christmases. May we hear it again and again.

What a night that would have been! With what "wondering awe" would we have searched the sky as the hours passed and the light grew as bright as noonday. We would have gathered our children around us and reverently taught them the meaning of a night with no darkness. We would have gathered in small groups of joy and happiness, almost not daring to believe what our eyes testified was true. Perhaps we would have sung the hymns of our belief. It would have been a night never to be forgotten.

With what emotion would we have greeted the rising sun after long hours of rejoicing? And when the star appeared, our wonder would have been born anew. I do not believe that an unlearned farm boy from New York could create such a story. I do not believe any kind of fiction could describe in such simple and undramatic language a moment, a time, a test, a faith, as sublime as the Nephite Christmas story. There *was* such a night of wonder and gratitude.

As a child I felt the wonder of Christmas in a worldly way. As a man the wonder has turned to a deep appreciation and reverence. It is my hope that we may feel this wonder all of our lives, especially on those nights when we watch the sunsets that settle the world into darkness.

S. Michael Wilcox is the author of To See His Face *and* Choosing the Fulness: Wickedness or Righteousness.

AWAY IN A MANGER

by Lael Littke

Nathaniel arrived at our house in September with a duffel bag and a supply of put-downs. "I hate it here," he announced immediately. He looked first at our surrounding fields, then at Laverne, me, Darwin, Rula Mae, Tootie, and Max, standing there in stair-step order of age. Last, he looked at our black-and-white dog, Sport, who as usual was nipping at his tail. "There's nothing here but cows and hayseeds and fleas," Nathaniel continued. "I wish I could go back home to New York City."

Within two days the rest of us kids wished the same thing. Nathaniel did nothing except complain and haunt the mailboxes out on the road, looking for a letter from his mother.

"She said she'd write soon and tell me when I can come home," he said every day.

And every day Darwin whispered, "I hope it comes soon."

"Well, now," Mama soothed, "your mother never was much of a letter writer, Nathaniel. You just be patient."

To us Mama said, "Be nice. He'll blend in eventually."

Nathaniel was the son of Aunt Delia, Mama's sister, who had run away with a rock singer when she was seventeen. The only things Mama had received from her in eleven years were a couple of phone calls and Nathaniel. The last phone call was about her getting married again, her third time. Soon after that Nathaniel arrived.

He was still with us at Christmastime, and we hoped that the season would work some kind of magic on him, like in the story about Scrooge. But Scrooge was a pushover compared to Nathaniel. When Mama started her Christmas baking, Nathaniel said he preferred the smell of hot pretzels in the New York subway. He said our little Christmas tree was nothing compared to the sky-tall wonder that was put up in Rockefeller Plaza each year. And, when we went to the nearby town of Pratt to do our Christmas shopping at the J.C. Penney store, he ruined our excitement by sneering, "You could put this whole hick town inside Macy's department store in New York City."

We were helping Mama make cookies on the day he told us about the store

10

windows in New York. "They have winter scenes with skaters on ponds and toy shops and whole towns right there in the windows, and *everything moves*."

The best our little village could do was a lighted plastic manger scene on the church lawn.

Laverne, who was rolling out cookie dough, put her chin up. "Well, here we go *caroling* and put on a *show* on Christmas Eve." She whacked at the dough with the rolling pin.

The caroling and the show were news to the rest of us kids. We had never done anything except make popcorn and maybe sing carols around the piano on Christmas Eve. We had only three neighbors within walking distance, and the snow was always deep at Christmas. We had never thought of going caroling.

"Oh?" Nathaniel said. "What kind of a show do you do?" He seemed interested, maybe because he was always saying he was going to be an actor on Broadway when he went home to New York.

"We do a *big* show." Laverne's eyes glazed over a little. "This year we're going to have Joseph and Mary and the Christ Child and costumes, and we'll read from the Bible. It will be the most wonderful Christmas show ever."

Rula Mae's face lit up. "I'll be Mary," she volunteered. "I can wear my long dress."

Rula Mae's most prized possession was a tattered chiffon formal Mama had worn, before any of us were born,

when she played the part of a society girl in a community play.

Laverne frowned. "That dress is *red*, with silver sequins all over the top. Mary wouldn't wear a dress like that."

"She would if she had one," Rula Mae said.

"When we put on Christmas shows in New York," Nathaniel said, "we always have a Mary dressed in blue robes. And a halo," he added, "that's lighted by radiant beams from heaven afar."

"You're making that up," Laverne said. "You got that from 'Silent Night.' "

"No, I didn't," Nathaniel said hotly. "The halo has *batteries*."

Laverne sniffed. "Well, our Mary is going to wear a red dress with a wreath of holly on her head." She jabbed at the rolled-out cookie dough with a cutter, making a row of big-winged angels. "Rula Mae, you can be Mary. And Darwin can be Joseph and wear his bathrobe for a costume. And Tootie can . . . "

"*Oh, no, I can't*," Darwin interrupted. "I'm not going *no* place in my bathrobe. Nathaniel can be Joseph."

"If I have to be in this hick show," Nathaniel said, "I'm going to be the Bible reader. I always got to be the reader in New York."

Darwin shrugged. "Then Max can be Joseph."

"That's *dumb*, Darwin," Laverne said. "Max is only two years old."

"Well, the only other guy we got is Sport." Darwin pointed at our dog who, on cue, sat down to nip at his tail.

Nathaniel groaned. "I'm not going to be in any stupid show where Joseph is biting fleas all the time."

Laverne scooped up angels with a spatula and slapped them onto a baking sheet. "Fine! I wanted to be the reader anyway. *You* can stay here and sulk."

"Be *nice*," Mama whispered.

Laverne sighed. "All *right*. Max will be Joseph. Jenny," she said to me, "you and Tootie can be angels. I'll be the shepherds watching their flocks, and Darwin can be the Three Wise Men." She sighed again. "Nathaniel, you can be the reader."

"Back in New York we had *multitudes* of angels," Nathaniel said.

Laverne ignored him and looked down at Tootie who was yanking at her sleeve. "Can we sing the songs about Harold and Gloria?" Tootie whispered.

The Harold and Gloria carols were Tootie's favorites. The year before she had named our two cats Harold and Gloria, and, when Gloria had two kittens, she named them Hark and Excelsis Deo. Later she gave Hark to our neighbors, the Nelsons, but we still had Excelsis Deo.

Laverne nodded. "We'll use all the good songs, Tootie."

"You ought to see the Christmas show at Radio City Music Hall in New York," Nathaniel said.

We didn't have many rehearsals because Max was always napping when the rest of us were available, but by Christmas Eve we were ready.

It was a cold night, and there had been snow flurries on and off all day. Rula Mae wanted to go without a coat to show off her red dress, but Mama said absolutely *not*. She made us all, including Rula Mae, wear coats and mittens and stocking caps. Nathaniel said that was a relief because Mary in a red sequined dress was really embarrassing. Laverne got mad and said that just because Mary wore blue robes in New York City there was no reason it *had* to be that way, and Mama whispered, "Be *nice*." Laverne gave a gusty sigh and told Rula Mae that people could still admire the *bottom* of her dress that showed under her coat, and Nathaniel said Mary certainly wouldn't wear a dress as tattered as the bottom part of that red dress was. Laverne yelled that Joseph and Mary were *poor*, for heaven's sake, and probably a tattered dress was no news to them.

"*Be nice!*" Mama said, not bothering to whisper this time.

Laverne sighed again as she pinned some tinsel along the sleeves of Tootie's and my coats and told us to flap our arms up and down when we were supposed to be angels. For her own shepherd costume she took a gunny sack and split it part way to make a hood. A few kernels of wheat fell out when she put it on her head. Nathaniel groaned.

Darwin insisted on wearing a pointed black hat Mama had made for Tootie when she was a witch in the second-grade Halloween play. He said that's what a wizard would wear, and he couldn't see any difference between a wizard and a Wise Man. He also said he was taking Sport along to be a camel. He said it didn't matter if camels had fleas.

Laverne got our emergency kerosene lantern from its shelf because she said it was more appropriate for our play than a flashlight.

When we were all ready to go, Nathaniel said, "We don't have a Baby Jesus."

"I'll get one," Tootie said. She brought forth Excelsis Deo and wrapped him in a blanket and laid him in an orange crate. The kitten must not have been theatrically inclined because he jumped out and ran away to the barn. We took the orange crate along with us anyway to be a manger bed.

We went first to the Blazers' house because they were the closest, and we were anxious for our debut. But their house was dark.

"They probably turned out the lights and hid when they saw us coming," Nathaniel muttered.

Nobody else said anything, and we went on through the deep snow to the Smiths' house. They were having a party. Nervously we set up our tableau by the light of the kerosene lantern.

When Max saw Darwin set down the orange crate, he crawled into it.

"You can't be in the manger bed," Rula Mae said. "You're supposed to be Joseph, Max." She tried to lift him out, but Max cried.

"Let him stay," Laverne said. "He can be the Baby Jesus instead of Joseph."

"He's too *big*," Nathaniel protested. "The Baby Jesus is a *little* baby, just born. He can't be sitting up like that."

Laverne put her hands on her hips. "Well, we can't have *everything* perfect. Now take your places and get ready."

She yanked Nathaniel over beside Rula Mae who sat in the snow, the shreds of her red skirt spread around her.

"Okay," Laverne said, "start singing. They'll all come out to watch."

She led us into "Away in a Manger," then Nathaniel read from Saint Luke. " 'And suddenly there was with the angel . . .' "

"Flap your arms, Tootie," Laverne said in a loud whisper.

" ' . . . A multitude of the heavenly host praising God, and saying, Glory to God in the highest.' "

We were halfway through "Hark, the Herald Angels Sing" when a man inside looked out through the window. We put new enthusiasm into our performance, but the man turned away. Nobody came out. None of us said anything as we completed our show.

We went on to the Nelsons' house where we set up our show outside the kitchen window. Inside we could see Mr. and Mrs. Nelson and their two teenage kids playing Monopoly.

"They don't want to watch us," Nathaniel said.

"Sing!" Laverne sounded cross.

" 'Away in a manger, no crib for a bed. . .' " Our voices crackled in the frosty air.

The kitchen door flew open. "What's

going on?" Mrs. Nelson bellowed.

Our song faltered to a stop.

"We came to put on a show for you," Laverne said.

"Well, thanks, but you'll catch your death of cold," Mrs. Nelson declared. "Go on home where it's warm."

"Ma," somebody yelled in the background, "do you want to buy Baltic Avenue or don't you?"

"Thanks for coming," Mrs. Nelson said, shutting the door.

We stared at the closed door. Sport barked at a shadow, but the rest of us didn't say a word as we gathered up the orange crate and started for home. It was snowing hard now, and the snow blew in our faces.

"Let's stop for a while in the Nelsons' barn," Laverne suggested. "Maybe the snow will let up."

Nathaniel groaned. "Wait till I tell the guys in New York that I spent Christmas Eve in a *barn*."

"Stay outside if you want to," Laverne told him.

"We don't care," Tootie said in her gentle little voice.

Rejection had made us all mean.

Nathaniel followed us inside.

Darwin, who carried the lantern, held it high. We walked into the center part of the barn where Mr. Nelson had thrown down hay from the loft above. Around us in the dim light we could see the eyes of the cows who placidly chewed their cuds. The horses in their stalls pricked their ears forward, and Hark, the kitten, came to the edge of the loft and looked down.

We burrowed into the hay and huddled close to get warm, except for Nathaniel who stood apart. Darwin set the lantern down in the hay, but Laverne snatched it up and hung it on a nail.

"You dummy," she said. "Do you want to burn the whole place down?"

"Sounds like a good idea," Nathaniel said. "That would be the most excitement I've had since I left New York City."

Laverne straightened up and moved close to Nathaniel. Something quivered in the air.

"That would make a Christmas like nothing you ever had in New York, wouldn't it?" she said softly. "You could tell your buddies about this whopper of a Christmas Eve out in the sticks when all the animals got fried just for your entertainment. You could tell them how Mr. Nelson lost all his equipment and how the neighbors came from miles around to see what they could do to help. Oh, it would be a really big party, Nathaniel. Too bad we can't provide you that pleasure before you go home." She paused for just a second. "But, to tell the truth, I don't think you're *ever* going home. I think you're stuck with us, Nathaniel, and we're stuck with you."

Her words kind of hung there in the air. She'd said something we had all suspected but had never laid tongue to.

Nathaniel's face kind of sagged, and he opened his mouth but didn't say anything. We knew that he knew.

There was silence in the barn, except for the munching of the animals, and

Hark, mewing in the loft above.

Nathaniel stood like an actor who has forgotten his lines. We all watched him, except for Max who sat in the orange crate, looking at the cows.

Suddenly Max began to sing, his reedy little voice cutting through the cold air. " 'Away in a manger, no cwib for a bed.' " Tootie joined in, then Darwin and I.

The cows stopped their chewing and a horse nickered in the night.

We finished the song. Nobody moved. Then Nathaniel cleared his throat. Stepping close to the lantern, he opened the Bible and read, " 'And it came to pass in those days, that there went out a decree from Caesar Augustus . . . .' " He sounded hoarse.

Hark jumped down from the loft and purred his way close to us. Sport sat down to scratch a flea, the thumping of his leg providing a background rhythm for Nathaniel's reading.

" 'And she brought forth her firstborn son, and wrapped him in swaddling clothes, and laid him in a manger; because there was no room for them in the inn.' "

Nathaniel's voice was feathery, like the falling snow outside.

" 'And suddenly there was with the angel . . .' " Tootie and I flapped our arms, and the ears of the cows snapped forward. " '. . . A multitude of the heavenly host praising God, and saying . . .' "

Now Nathaniel's voice was big, and the way he read the words we could almost believe there *was* a multitude.

" 'Glo-o-o-o-oria, in excelsis deo,' " we all sang. Rula Mae's face was serene as she sat there in the hay in her red sequined dress. Darwin gazed at the animals, and Laverne knelt beside the orange crate.

Our audience was quiet. Attentive. Their hairy faces reflected back the light of the lantern. We finished our show, and there was no applause except for the measured breathing of the patient beasts.

We stayed where we were for what seemed like a long time. Then Laverne stood up and walked over to Nathaniel.

"That was good, Nathaniel," she said. "I can see why you were always the reader in New York."

Nathaniel looked around him. "This was the best I ever did." He brushed a hand across his eyes. "And next year I'll do it even better." He straightened his shoulders and took a deep breath.

We gathered our things together, then moved in close to Nathaniel as we went out into the snowy night.

Lael Littke has published several young-adult novels, including Where the Creeks Meet *and* Shanny on Her Own, *which was chosen as a Junior Literary Guild selection in 1985. Her feature stories have appeared in over seventy-five magazines, including* McCall's, Seventeen, *and* Good Housekeeping. *"Away In a Manger,"* © *1986 by McCall's Publishing Co. Reprinted by permission of Larry Sternig Literary Agency.*

A CHRISTMAS SONG

by Jack Weyland

My mother died in March, not from the arthritis she fought for several years but from pneumonia. I didn't even know someone could get pneumonia that way. I mean, she hardly ever left our home.

They say the hardest time to get through after something like that happens is the first Christmas. I guess that's true. It's like a complicated puzzle somebody gives you that you never wanted. You work on it hour after hour but never solve it. My thoughts keep going back to last Christmas—sorting through each detail, measuring each gesture, weighing every word. Lately I've been trying to remember what I gave her for Christmas, but I can't. But I do remember what she gave me.

Arthritis is a slow disease. From day to day there doesn't seem to be any change. I don't even know exactly when it began, maybe four or five years ago. During that time it took my mother's hands and deformed the joints, and bent her neck so she couldn't hold her head erect, and weakened her knees so she couldn't walk.

At first Dad and I had hope about her getting well. They're doing lots of research, we thought, and any time they might find a cure. Besides, there were always people talking about a relative who ate sunflower seeds or drank goat's milk and was cured.

"I wouldn't mind being sick," my mother would say, "if I could look pretty at the same time." She was pretty once. Sometimes I look at my parents' picture taken outside the Salt Lake Temple when they were married. My mother looks so young in the picture. My dad has dark hair and is still lean. Of course, now he's lost most of his hair and put on a little weight around the belt.

There's something strange about that picture. All over the temple grounds, except on the sidewalk where it's been shoveled, there is newly fallen snow. But my mother in her white wedding gown is holding a large bunch of lilac blossoms in her arms. It must have been a late spring snowstorm that came after the lilacs had bloomed. I wish I had asked her about the lilacs.

After the disease started to win, my mother had Dad take down the mirror

17

in the hall so she wouldn't see herself when we wheeled her from the bedroom into the living room. She weighed less than ninety pounds.

My mother was a good musician. She was in charge of the ward choir as far back as I can remember. She also played the piano in Primary. When anyone wanted a special number in sacrament meeting, they would call her and she'd arrange it. Every Christmas she would get music together for a special presentation. But a year before she died, she had to ask to be released because of the arthritis.

Last year at this time I was a senior in high school. Kara Erickson and I went together to most of the ward activities. We weren't really going steady, but in our ward there weren't many others our age. And we liked each other.

One Wednesday near Christmas during activity night they turned the time over to Sister Robbins. She and her husband had just moved from Utah, where they had both been going to school.

"The bishop has asked me to be in charge of a special youth vocal number for the program before Christmas. What do you want to sing?"

There were a few groans from the Scouts.

" 'Silent Night,' " one of the Beehive girls said.

"That's too slow," someone else complained.

"Yea, something that doesn't drag."

"Christmas is such a happy time.

Let's do something with some life to it, like 'Deck the Halls.' "

I got up and walked out into the hall and waited for them to finish singing so I could go to class. Somehow I felt depressed that they would have Christmas music without my mother there to help.

Later I drove Kara home.

There's something you should know about Kara. She's really beautiful and smart and everything, but in high school she didn't get asked out as much as you'd expect. One day in early morning seminary we were talking about dating. We were both sixteen. She told the class that she had decided she wasn't going to date nonmembers and she wasn't going to kiss any guy until she was sure she loved him enough to marry him. Some of the kids in the class thought that was dumb about not kissing. But she wouldn't change her mind.

There aren't that many LDS guys in our small Montana town. By the time we were both seniors, I was the only one dating her, although we never decided to go steady.

After I had been dating Kara for a long time, guys at school would come up to me and ask, "You mean you've never even kissed her once?"

"No."

"I don't believe it. That's not normal."

Of course, I would have liked to kiss her. But sometimes I wonder if we weren't closer that way. I mean we talked a lot. And I began to see how lucky the guy would be who did marry her.

But that night I wasn't very good company. We pulled up in front of her house and stopped.

"Steve, Sister Robbins was asking about you. Why didn't you stay for the practice?"

"I didn't feel like singing."

"She really needs you. She only has two others singing bass."

"I won't sing."

"She's got some arrangements of things they did at BYU. She says it's going to be the best ever."

"It was the best when my mother led the singing."

Another thing about Kara and me — we ended our dates with prayer. We didn't tell anybody about that. They would have really laughed.

We got two weeks of vacation from school for Christmas. At the same time the lady who stayed with my mother during the day asked for time off to visit her sister in Kansas. Dad asked me if I would stay home during the days of my vacation to help Mother.

Each day of the vacation seemed much like the one before. When she woke up I lifted her out of bed into the wheelchair. I helped her wash up, getting the washcloth wet with warm water, putting soap on it, and handing it to her. When she was finished, I rinsed it out, let her get the soap off, and handed her a towel. Eventually we got to the kitchen, and I fixed her something to eat. After breakfast I got her some aspirin and a Darvon. Then I

wheeled her into the living room and turned on the TV. It didn't really matter what was on. Just anything to take her mind off the pain. About 11:00 the mail came. At noon I fixed her lunch. In the afternoon she tried to walk. I stood beside her and held onto her, and she put one foot a couple of inches in front of the other and slowly moved forward. After going a couple of feet she was exhausted, and I put her on the couch so she could rest.

Thursday before Christmas she had an appointment with the doctor. My dad came home from work early. He moved the car into the driveway, opening the right front door. Then he came inside and picked her up in his arms and carried her to the car.

As he began to slide her into the front seat, he stumbled a little. Her legs hit the door post.

"You clumsy!" she screamed at him. "Can't you see you're hurting me?"

On the way to the doctor my mother cried, first from the pain, and then because she'd said that to my dad. But he understood how it was for her.

When we got home after the appointment, Dad carried Mother into the bedroom and let her rest. Then he had to go back to work.

I turned on the TV. There was something secure about sitting there. It was as if I could plug my mind into it and let it guide me so I'd never have to remember my mother screaming with pain.

Later I went to our bookshelf and looked a long time at my parents' wedding picture. I wondered what my dad would have done if somehow before the wedding he had been told that twenty years later that young girl beside him would turn brittle. And I wondered what disease might be locked up inside Kara—or myself.

That night I had to get away, so I took Kara to the movies. The movie was as depressing as the day had been. After the movie I took her right home. As soon as the car stopped I opened the door and went around to the other side to let her out.

"Aren't we going to pray together tonight?"

"Don't ask that tonight. Just go inside."

"Steve, please."

"Okay," I said harshly. "Will you offer it?"

She knew I felt rotten, and she was trying to help. "Could we kneel? We could go in the backyard by the trees."

"Whatever you say," I said angrily. We walked out into her backyard.

When we got to the place, isolated by some trees, she knelt down. I stood there looking at her, unable to make myself kneel down. "I can't, Kara. You go ahead."

"Why can't you pray?"

"God doesn't listen to me anymore," I said with bitterness.

"He loves you, Steve."

"No, not me. The only thing I've ever asked him is that my mother would get better. Kara, she's getting worse. But you go ahead. Don't let me stop you. Pray for good health for your

family. God listens to you."

"Don't say those things," she said, hurt and disappointed.

"Well, go ahead and pray if you want to pray!" I yelled at her.

She began to cry. After a few minutes that seemed a hundred years in which I couldn't seem to force myself to move or help her, I finally broke loose and helped her to her feet. I took a tissue and wiped away the tears I had caused.

"I'm sorry. I didn't mean to take it out on you," I said.

"I know. It's not easy for you at home."

We walked into the front yard. The Christmas tree lights glowed delicately from the living room window. I could see Kara's mother busy sewing a dress.

"Merry Christmas," I said grimly. "Are there really people on the earth who have a merry Christmas? I'm so afraid of Christmas this year. I wish I could take a pill and go to sleep and not wake up until January."

"Steve, if you would sing with us Sunday, it would be good for you."

"No, the words would choke me. My mother used to do so much in music that it would haunt me. You go ahead. I'm sure it will be fine. Just don't ask me to sing."

Friday morning was the same as Thursday morning. There were a lot of Christmas movies on television. I saw *White Christmas* with Bing Crosby three times that week.

In the afternoon my mother slept for about an hour. When she woke up, I got her a glass of milk with brewer's yeast in it.

"What time is it?" she asked.

"Three o'clock."

"Can you change it to channel four?"

I got up and changed the channel. There was a documentary on fish farms in the South.

"Are you sure you're on channel four? It's supposed to be 'Search for Tomorrow.' "

"It's the right channel. Do you want me to leave it there?"

"If they say they're going to show something at a certain time, why don't they show it?"

"I don't know. What do you want me to do?"

"Change over to channel seven," she said.

"Do you want that?" I asked, looking at a program on French cooking.

"I don't know what I want," she said numbly. "Turn back to channel four, but turn the volume down so we'll know if 'Search for Tomorrow' comes on. Do you think I should take some aspirin? What time is it?"

"A little after three."

"I guess I'll wait so they'll be still working when your dad comes home. Can you put me in the wheelchair and roll me out by the window?"

I pushed her next to our picture window. "Still no snow," she said, looking out at the grays and browns. "It doesn't seem much like Christmas, does it?"

"No."

"A few years ago I'd be busy now getting ready for the musical program on Sunday. Do you remember when we sang parts from the *Messiah?* We invited the whole town. One year we had the Primary children sing the whole program. Once we even had a string quartet. I wonder if anyone in the ward remembers that."

I said that they did, although people move in and out of our ward so fast that I doubted if very many people were still here that were here then.

"I've been away for so long. I don't even know the people in the choir now. Have you met Sister Robbins? Kara's mother told me she's the choir leader now. I bet they'll be singing this Sunday. Will you tell me how it goes?"

"I'm not going."

"Steve, you've never missed before."

"I'll go to Livingston for church, but I'm not going to our ward. Don't ask me to do it. I wish it were over."

"What's wrong?"

"When they sing, I'll be sad that you're not up there singing. In the talks someone will get up and say what great blessings he's received. Well, we live the gospel and you're sick. Where are our blessings?"

"Steve, I've never heard you talk like that."

"It's just Christmas. I'll be okay after it's over."

I know that really bothered her. Maybe I shouldn't have said it. I guess if I had known she was going to die in a few months, I would have held my tongue. But I didn't know that.

I sat down, turned up the TV, and

tried to plug my mind into its security.

After a few minutes, during a commercial, I got up and rolled her back to her chair. I got her an aspirin, a Darvon pill, and a glass of water, and then sat down and watched "Lucy."

After "Lucy" there was the "Brady Bunch."

"Steve, turn the TV off."

I turned it off.

"Do you remember when we used to make special cookies for Christmas? Why don't you and I make some now? We'll surprise your dad when he comes home. It'll be just like it used to be."

I rolled her into the kitchen. She seemed excited about making the cookies. She told what to do, helping me find the recipe, telling me where the cookie cutters were so we could make Christmas trees, Santa Clauses, and stars. She said she'd cut out the shapes after we'd finished with the dough.

I started on the recipe, adding each ingredient as it was listed.

"A cup of sugar," I read, going to the cupboard.

"That's not enough."

"It says one cup."

"I changed the recipe. I put in more sugar."

"How much more?"

"I can't remember."

"How about if I put in a cup and follow the recipe?"

"It won't taste the same as it did on other Christmases."

"Nothing about this Christmas is the same," I thought to myself.

After I finished mixing the cookie

dough, I put down some waxed paper on the table and rolled the dough out.

My mother wanted to help with the cookies to please Dad. She picked up one of the cookie cutters and placed it on the dough and pressed. Although she made an indentation in the dough, she couldn't seem to push hard enough to actually cut out the shape. She tried it again. I wanted to help her, but she wanted to do it herself so Dad would be proud.

Suddenly she just quit. "I can't do it. I can't do anything. There's nothing I can do. I'm no good to anyone."

I picked up the dough, ran with it to the disposal, and got rid of it.

I pushed her back to the living room. Tears rolled down her cheeks. She couldn't use her hands very well to stop them, and so they streamed down and fell from her face.

We turned on the TV and sat there silently watching a documentary on raising African violets. After that we watched "Password."

"Steve, I don't want to watch any more TV." I turned it off.

"What is this disease doing to us?" she asked. "You asked where our blessings were. Don't you know?"

"I want you to be well. That's all I want. Why can't God hear me?"

"I used to wonder that, too. He hears us. But if he rewarded everyone who loved him with good health and everyone who disobeyed him with sickness, who wouldn't follow him? But then there would be no agency. The glory of the gospel is that even in pain we can maintain our faith. This is not going to defeat me. I'm going to fight it all the way. And someday I'll walk."

I looked at her weak legs, feeling she'd never walk, and said weakly, "Sure you will."

"I will. If not here in this life, then in the next. I've memorized a scripture. 'For I know that my redeemer liveth, and that he shall stand at the latter day upon the earth. And though after my skin worms destroy this body, yet in my flesh shall I see God.'

"I'll see him. I'll stand. I'll walk again. Because of the Savior, I'll stand."

She had never talked to me like that before.

"Steve, when I dream in the night, I dream I'm walking. I'll walk again. Your dad and I have been through the temple. We've tried to do the best we could. I want so much to stand some-day beside your father and be with him in the celestial kingdom, not with this deformed body, but with a body that can stand tall and walk. That hope is one of my greatest blessings. Don't you understand?"

I nodded my head.

"Can we have a prayer before your dad comes home so he won't have to bear any more burden than he has al-ready?"

"I can't pray, Mom. I don't even know what to ask for anymore."

"Please, son, honor your priest-hood."

"Father in heaven, please help us get through Christmas with some happi-ness. In Jesus' name. Amen."

My dad came home about 5:00. I helped him cook supper. After that we took out our plastic tree, assembled it, and put a few ornaments on it. We put our presents under the tree. Then we sat down and watched TV.

About 8:00 we heard some car doors slam, and in a minute our doorbell rang. My dad opened the door.

It was Sister Robbins, Kara, and a bunch of kids from church.

"Could I talk to your wife?" Sister Robbins asked.

"I'm sorry to bother you like this, but we need your help. We're supposed to put on a part for the Christmas pro-gram on Sunday, and I'm afraid I've gotten in over my head. The kids told me you used to do this all the time. I was wondering if you'd mind listening to us and giving your suggestions."

They got around the piano and began to sing. When they finished, my mother gave some ideas to help it. We sang another song. You should have seen my mother. The body was de-formed, the old pale robe hiding weak and spindly arms and legs. But her eyes came alive. She listened and helped with such enthusiasm. Before long she had us singing parts.

I've found out since then that Sister Robbins is really a good musician. I'm not sure she needed as much help as she said she did. That night she asked my mother about every little thing. My mother lit up. The more she helped, the more spirit came into her face.

"Why didn't I think of that?" Sister Robbins said at one point.

"Well, remember, I've had twenty years working on choirs."

While they talked I went into the kitchen. Kara was talking to my dad while they both set out plates and glasses.

"Your dad says you're becoming quite a help in the kitchen."

"He'll make somebody a fine husband," my dad said with a grin. "After his mission, that is," he added.

Kara set out a fresh batch of Christmas cookies she had made that afternoon. She had planned the whole thing with Sister Robbins. She was the way in which Heavenly Father answered my prayer.

We had cookies and milk. After that we sang more Christmas songs. My mother led us with nods of her head.

Of course, I sang with the choir that Sunday. My dad brought my mother to church long enough to partake of the sacrament and listen to the musical numbers, and then the pain got too bad for her, and he had to take her home.

When I remember my mother, I can't altogether forget the pain she had or the savage way arthritis dealt with her. That's a part of my life.

My thoughts often go back to the picture of her as a young bride holding those lilacs in the midst of all that snow. At the same time I remember her saying, "I'll stand. I'll walk again. Because of the Savior, I'll stand!"

That's what she gave me for our last Christmas. Somehow I think that is what she would want me to remember.

Jack Weyland is the author of a number of best-selling novels, including Brenda at the Prom, Charly, Sam, Sara, Whenever I Hear Your Name, PepperTide, The Understudy, *and* Last of the Big-Time Spenders; *three collections of short stories, including* A Small Light in the Darkness; *and a book on self-esteem,* If Talent Were Pizza, You'd Be a Supreme. *"A Christmas Song" was previously published in the* New Era.

MAYBE CHRISTMAS DOESN'T COME FROM A STORE

by Jeffrey R. Holland

You will recall from Dr. Seuss's holiday horror story, *How the Grinch Stole Christmas,* that the devilish Grinch determined to rob Who-ville of every holiday treat. In a nefarious scheme in which the Grinch dressed as Santa himself, he moved through Who-ville taking every package, tree, ornament, and stocking.

As he left the city with his sack full of stolen gifts, he chuckled in delight over the pain his actions would cause the people of Who-ville. He climbed to the top of a mountain where he anxiously waited to hear the sound of youthful anguish coming from the city below. He even cupped his hand to his ear in eager anticipation.

But what he heard instead were the joyful sounds of happy people celebrating Christmas. He was chagrined—and amazed. He couldn't imagine it, but Christmas had arrived in spite of himself! Though the people of Who-ville had no trees to trim, no ornaments to enjoy, no packages to unwrap, they were having a wonderful Christmas anyway. It was more than the Grinch could fathom.

And he puzzled three hours, till his puzzler was sore.
Then the Grinch thought of something he hadn't before!
"Maybe Christmas," he thought, *"doesn't* come from a store.
"Maybe Christmas . . . perhaps . . . means a little bit more!"
(Dr. Seuss, *How the Grinch Stole Christmas,* New York: Random House, 1957. Used with permission.)

Part of the purpose for telling the story of Christmas is to remind us that Christmas doesn't come from a store. Indeed, however delightful we feel about it, even as children, each year it "means a little bit more." And no matter how many times we read the biblical account of that evening in Bethlehem, we always come away with a thought—or two—we haven't had before.

There are so many lessons to be learned from the sacred account of Christ's birth that we always hesitate to emphasize one at the expense of all the others. Forgive me while I do just that.

One impression which has persisted with me is that this is a story—in profound paradox with our own times—of intense poverty. I wonder if Luke did not have some special meaning when he wrote *not* that "there was no room in the inn" but specifically that "there was no room *for them* in the inn." (Luke 2:7; italics added.) We cannot be certain, but it is my guess that money could talk in those days as well as in our own. I think if Joseph and Mary had been people of influence or means, they would have found lodging even at that busy time of year.

I have wondered if the Inspired Version also was suggesting they did not know the "right people" in saying, "There was none to give room for them in the inns." (JST, Luke 2:7.)

We cannot be certain what the historian intended, but we *do* know these two were desperately poor. At the purification offering which the parents made after the child's birth, a turtle-dove was substituted for the required lamb, a substitution the Lord had allowed in the Law of Moses to ease the burden of the truly impoverished. (See Leviticus 12:8.)

The wise men did come later bearing gifts, adding some splendor and wealth to this occasion, but it is important to note that they came from a distance, probably Persia, a trip of several hundred miles at the very least. Unless they started long before the star appeared, it is highly unlikely that they arrived on the night of the Babe's birth.

Indeed, Matthew records that when they came Jesus was a "young child," and the family was living in a "house." (Matthew 2:11.)

Perhaps this provides an important distinction we should remember in our own holiday season. Maybe the purchasing and the making and the wrapping and the decorating—those delightfully generous and important expressions of our love at Christmas—should be separated, if only slightly, from the more quiet, personal moments when we consider the meaning of the Baby (and His birth) who prompts the giving of such gifts.

As happens so often if we are not careful, the symbols can cover that which is symbolized. In some of our lives the manger has already been torn down to allow for a discount store running three-for-a-dollar specials on gold, frankincense, and myrrh.

I do not feel—or mean this to sound—like a modern-day Scrooge. The gold, frankincense, and myrrh were humbly given and appreciatively received, and so they should be, every year and always. As my wife and children can testify, no one gets more giddy about the giving and receiving of presents than I do.

But for that very reason, I, like you, need to remember the very plain scene, even the poverty, of a night devoid of tinsel or wrapping or goods of this world. Only when we see that single, sacred, unadorned object of our devotion—the Babe of Bethlehem—will we know why " 'tis the season to be jolly" and why the giving of gifts is so appropriate.

As a father I have recently begun to think more often of Joseph, that strong, silent, almost unknown man who must have been more worthy than any other mortal man to be the guiding foster father of the living Son of God. It was Joseph selected from among all men who would teach Jesus to work. It was Joseph who taught Him the books of the law. It was Joseph who, in the seclusion of the shop, helped Him begin to understand who He was and ultimately what He was to become.

I was a student at BYU just finishing my first year of graduate work when our first child, a son, was born. We were very poor, though not so poor as Joseph and Mary. My wife and I were both going to school, both holding jobs, and in addition worked as head residents in an off-campus apartment complex to help defray our rent. We drove a little Volkswagen which had a half-dead battery because we couldn't afford a new one (Volkswagen *or* battery).

Nevertheless, when I realized that our own night of nights was coming, I believe I would have done any honorable thing in this world, and mortgaged any future I had, to make sure my wife had the clean sheets, the sterile utensils, the attentive nurses, and the skilled doctors who brought forth our firstborn son. If she or that child had needed special care at the Mayo Clinic, I believe I would have ransomed my very life to get it.

I compare those feelings (which I have had with each succeeding child) with what Joseph must have felt as he moved through the streets of a city not his own, with not a friend or kinsman in sight, or anyone willing to extend a helping hand. In these very last and most painful hours of her "confinement," Mary had ridden or walked approximately one hundred miles from Nazareth in Galilee to Bethlehem in Judea. Surely Joseph must have wept at her silent courage. Now, alone and unnoticed, they had to descend from human company to a stable, a grotto full of animals, there to bring forth the Son of God.

I wonder what emotions Joseph might have had as he cleared away the dung and debris. I wonder if he felt the sting of tears as he hurriedly tried to find the cleanest straw and hold the animals back. I wonder if he wondered: "Could there be a more unhealthy, a more disease-ridden, a more despicable circumstance in which a child could be born? Is this a place fit for a king? Should the mother of the Son of God be asked to enter the valley of the shadow of death in such a foul and unfamiliar place as this? Is it wrong to wish her some comfort? Is it right He should be born here?"

But I am certain Joseph did not mutter and Mary did not wail. They knew a great deal and did the best they could.

Perhaps these parents knew even then that in the beginning of His mortal life, as well as in the end, this baby son born to them would have to descend beneath every human pain and disappointment. He would do so to help those who also felt they had been born without advantage.

I've thought of Mary, too, this most favored mortal woman in the history of the world, who as a mere child received an angel who uttered to her those words that would change the course not only of her own life but also that of all human history: "Hail, thou virgin, who art highly favoured of the Lord. The Lord is with thee; for thou art chosen and blessed among women." (JST, Luke 1:28.) The nature of her spirit and the depth of her preparation were revealed in a response that shows both innocence and maturity: "Behold the handmaid of the Lord; be it unto me according to thy word." (Luke 1:38.)

It is here I stumble, here that I grasp for the feelings a mother has when she knows she has conceived a living soul, feels life quicken and grow within her womb, and carries a child to delivery. At such times fathers stand aside and watch, but mothers feel and never forget. Again, I've thought of Luke's careful phrasing about that holy night in Bethlehem:

"The days were accomplished that *she* . . . . brought forth *her* firstborn son, and [*she*] wrapped him in swaddling clothes, and [*she*] laid him in a manger." (Luke 2:6-7; italics added.) Those brief pronouns trumpet in our ears that, second only to the child himself, Mary is the chiefest figure, the regal queen, mother of mothers—holding center stage in this grandest of all dramatic moments. And those same pro-

nouns also trumpet that, save for her beloved husband, she was very much alone.

I have wondered if this young woman, something of a child herself, here bearing her first baby, might have wished her mother, or an aunt, or her sister, or a friend, to be near her through the labor. Surely the birth of such a son as this should command the aid and attention of every midwife in Judea. We all might wish that someone could have held her hand, cooled her brow, and when the ordeal was over, given her rest in crisp, cool linen.

But it was not to be so. With only Joseph's inexperienced assistance, she herself brought forth her firstborn son, wrapped him in the little clothes she had knowingly brought on her journey, and perhaps laid him on a pillow of hay.

Then, on both sides of the veil, a heavenly host broke into song. "Glory to God in the highest," they sang, "and on earth, peace among men of good will." (Luke 2:14, Phillips Translation.) But except for heavenly witnesses, these three were alone: Joseph, Mary, the baby to be named Jesus.

At this focal point of all human history, a point illuminated by a new star in the heavens revealed for just such a purpose, probably no other mortal watched—none but a poor young carpenter, a beautiful virgin mother, and silent stabled animals who had not the power to utter the sacredness they had seen.

Shepherds would soon arrive and,

later, wise men from the East. Later yet the memory of that night would bring Santa Claus and Frosty and Rudolph—and all would be welcome. But first and forever there was just a little family, without toys or trees or tinsel. With a baby—that's how Christmas began.

It is for this baby that we shout in chorus: "Hark! the herald angels sing Glory to the newborn King! . . . Mild he lays his glory by, Born that man no more may die; Born to raise the sons of earth, Born to give them second birth." (*Hymns*, Salt Lake City: The Church of Jesus Christ of Latter-day Saints, 1985, no. 209.)

Perhaps recalling the circumstances of that gift, of His birth, of His own childhood, perhaps remembering that purity and faith and genuine humility will be required of every celestial soul, Jesus must have said many times as He looked into the little eyes that loved Him (eyes that always best saw what and who He really was), "Except ye be converted, and become as little children, ye shall not enter into the kingdom of heaven." (Matthew 18:3.)

Christmas, then, is for children—of all ages. I suppose that is why my favorite Christmas carol is a child's song. I sing it with more emotion than any other:

> Away in a manger, no crib for his bed,
> The little Lord Jesus laid down his sweet head. . . .
> I love thee, Lord Jesus; look down from the sky
> And stay by my cradle till morning is nigh.
> Be near me, Lord Jesus, I ask thee to stay
> Close by me forever, and love me, I pray.
> Bless all the dear children in thy tender care,
> And fit us for heaven to live with thee there.
> (*Hymns*, no. 206.)

"Then the Grinch thought of something he hadn't before! 'Maybe Christmas,' he thought, '*doesn't* come from a store.' "

Jeffrey R. Holland is the president of Brigham Young University. His previously published works include However Long and Hard the Road. *This article was first published in the* Ensign, December 1977.

REFLECTIONS ON
THE CHRISTMAS STORY

by Gerald N. Lund

"And in the sixth month the angel Gabriel was sent from God unto a city of Galilee, named Nazareth." (Luke 1:26.)

The rabbis of ancient Israel had a saying: "Judea is wheat, Galilee straw, beyond Jordan, only chaff."[1] The urbane and worldly wise Jerusalemite, privileged to dwell in the Holy City, looked down on all others with faint condescension; but they especially viewed the Galileans as crude, unlearned, and earthy peasants. For the most part the people of Galilee were men of the soil and of the sea. This kept them in touch with basic values; and in spite of the feelings of the Judeans, they were known for being hard-working and warm-hearted, and for showing unrestrained hospitality and uncompromising honesty.

As for Nazareth itself, like many other villages of Judea and Galilee, it sat amid steep, tree-covered hillsides so as not to utilize precious agricultural land. For a village now so famous to us, it seems to have been of singular insignificance then. It is not even mentioned in the Old Testament or in the extensive writings of the ancient historian Josephus. Nathanael expressed what must have been a common feeling even among the Galileans when he said, "Can there any good thing come out of Nazareth?" (John 1:46.) Evidently, the suggestion that the Messiah had come from such a civic backwater was unthinkable.

But that is not to say that this home village of Mary and Joseph, and later the Master Himself, was a drab and dull setting. One writer describes it as follows: "You cannot see from Nazareth the surrounding country, for Nazareth lies in a basin; but the moment you climb to the edge of the basin . . . what a view you have. Esdraelon lies before you, with its twenty battlefields. . . . There is Naboth's vineyard and the place of Jehu's revenge upon Jezebel; there Shunem and the house of Elisha; the Carmel and the place of Elijah's sacrifice. To the east the valley of Jordan, . . . to the west the radiance of the Great Sea. . . . You can see thirty miles in three directions."[2]

This was the setting in which our story begins.

"To a virgin espoused to a man whose

30

name was Joseph, of the house of David." (Luke 1:27.)

As we are dropped into the midst of their lives, Joseph and Mary are "espoused." (Matthew 1:18.) Espousal among the Hebrews was significantly more binding than are our engagements today. It was entered into by written agreement and was considered the formal beginning of the marriage itself. While the couple might not actually live together for as much as a year after the betrothal—a time designed to allow the bride to prepare her dowry—the espousal was as legally binding as the formal marriage.

No hint of the age of either Mary or Joseph is given in the scriptural text, but from existing sources we can make some educated guesses. We know that puberty began somewhat earlier in the Middle East than is common in Western countries today. Therefore, marriage at earlier ages than to which we are accustomed was the general rule. Speaking of men, one rabbi described the stages of development as follows: At five he began study of Torah; at ten, study of the Mishnah (the oral laws); at fifteen, the study of Talmud (the extensive commentaries on the scriptures); *at eighteen,* marriage; at twenty, he pursued a trade or business and so on.[3] For a girl, probably the most common age of marriage was fifteen or sixteen. Sometimes it was later, sometimes earlier, but it is likely that Mary was around sixteen and Joseph, her espoused husband, only two or three years older than that.

Nazareth was a small village. Joseph and Mary must have known each other well. How fascinating it would be to know the circumstances that brought them to the point of betrothal. Much is made of the fact that in those days marriages were arranged by the families through the auspices of a matchmaker. No doubt that was true, but that does not mean that the individuals involved had no voice in the matter. We know from contemporary sources that, once the arrangements were made, the consent of the couple was required. The man had a direct say in the choice of his bride, and the woman could refuse the marital arrangements if not to her satisfaction.[4] So what was it that drew these two together?

We know Mary must have been of unusual loveliness. Nephi saw her in vision six hundred years before her birth and described her as "exceedingly fair" and "most beautiful and fair." (1 Nephi 11:13, 15.) But was it only the outward beauty Joseph saw, or did he sense the same qualities that caused Gabriel to declare that this woman was "highly favoured" of the Lord? (Luke 1:28.) No wonder Joseph loved her! Imagine finding a woman of such remarkable grace and beauty in a small village in the mountains of the Galilee.

And what of Joseph? What was it about this man that caused Mary to give her consent to the marriage arrangements? Only a few scriptural verses tell us about Joseph. He was a carpenter, that we know. (See Matthew 13:55.) And because fathers commonly

taught their sons their own trade, it is likely that Joseph was raised in a carpenter's shop at the knee of his father. His hands would have been rough and callused. He was a man of labor, a man who created things through his own craftsmanship.

Matthew also describes him as a "just man." (Matthew 1:19.) It is a simple phrase, yet it speaks volumes, for those same words are used to describe men such as Noah, Job, Nephi, and Jacob. Was it purely by accident that such a man was in Nazareth waiting to be Mary's partner in this most significant of dramas? Surely God the Father had seen in Joseph a man worthy to raise His Son and help prepare Him for His mortal ministry. While it would not be Joseph's privilege to actually father the "Firstborn," it would be his labor that would provide for His needs, his voice that would encourage His first steps, his hands that would guide the boy's fingers across the sacred scrolls of the Torah in those first Hebrew lessons. It was also Joseph who would put a mallet and chisel and plane in those smaller hands so that one day this boy from Nazareth would also be known as "the carpenter." (Mark 6:3.) No wonder Mary loved him!

"And the virgin's name was Mary." (Luke 1:27.)

One of the most common feminine names in the New Testament is Mary, or *Miryam* (Miriam) in Hebrew. One Bible concordance identifies at least seven different Marys in the New Testament, so it is not surprising to find a virgin of that name in the village of Nazareth.[5] But perhaps there is more to it than that. Among the Book of Mormon prophets, even a hundred years before the birth of the Savior, the actual name of the woman who was to mother the Messiah was known: It was to be Mary. (See Mosiah 3:8; Alma 7:10.) If that was so among Book of Mormon prophets, is it not possible that it was also known among Old Testament prophets as well, and therefore among the people of the Holy Land?

We know from existing records that the people at the time of Christ's birth generally believed that the birth of the long-awaited Messiah was imminent. What mother would not hope that her daughter might be the promised vessel for such an honor? Such maternal optimism might explain the frequency with which daughters were named Mary at this period of time. But for whatever reason, Mary's mother fulfilled prophetic promises when she named her child, little dreaming that it would indeed be her daughter that would do so.

"And the angel came in unto her, and said, Hail, thou that art highly favoured, the Lord is with thee: blessed art thou among women. And when she saw him, she was troubled at his saying, and cast in her mind what manner of salutation this should be. And the angel said unto her, Fear not, Mary: for thou hast found favour with God. And, behold, thou shalt conceive in thy womb, and bring forth a son, and shalt call his name Jesus." (Luke 1:28-31.)

It was August in Galilee.[6] The heat, even at night, can be stifling and oppressive. Luke indicates that Mary and Joseph were likely of poor families.[7] If that be the case, the house of Mary's family would have been small, no more than one or two rooms curtained off for sleeping and privacy at night. We are not told if it was day or night, or if she was alone in the house; surely she must have felt a sudden clutch of fear when she looked up and saw a personage standing there before her. All of us have had someone come up behind us, or appear in a doorway unexpectedly and startle us. We give an involuntary cry of surprise and feel the quick burst of adrenalin that leaves the heart pounding, the palms sweaty, and the mouth dry. So it is not difficult to imagine the shock of having not just a man appear suddenly in your room, but a being of transcendent radiance and glory.

But the shock of Gabriel's sudden appearance could not have been any greater than the stunning impact of his words. First there was the "impossible" announcement that she was about to conceive. Her response is so spontaneous, so logical. It adds even further to the power and simplicity with which Luke tells us of this night. One can almost picture her blurting it out, in spite of the glory of the being that stood before her: "How shall this be, seeing I know not a man?" (Luke 1:34.)

But that was only the first of the stunning pronouncements. The Messiah had been foretold for four millennia. Now to realize that the long centuries of waiting had come to end, that the Messiah was about to be born, and she—Mary of Nazareth—was to be the mother! Add to that the declaration that, for the first and only time in the history of the world, this was to be a virgin birth, and the revelation was even more staggering. This simple, pure woman from a little-known city in Galilee was to carry in her womb the divine offspring of the great Elohim Himself. Her son would also be the Son of God!

Only when we consider the magnitude of those statements do we begin to appreciate how marvelous is Mary's answer. There were no questioning looks, no stammering demands of "Why me?" There were no murmurs of doubt. There was no disputation, no hesitation, no wondering. She simply said, in glorious and touching simplicity: "Behold the handmaid of the Lord; be it unto me according to thy word." (Luke 1:38.)

"Now the birth of Jesus Christ was on this wise: When as his mother Mary was espoused to Joseph, before they came together, she was found with child of the Holy Ghost." (Matthew 1:18.)

At the command of great Gabriel, Mary left Nazareth to visit her cousin Elizabeth, wife of Zacharias the priest, living in Judea, now six months pregnant with a miracle of her own. There Mary abode with her kinswoman about three months until it was time for Elizabeth to deliver.

Consider for a moment what it must have meant for Mary to come back to Nazareth at that point. She suddenly, unexpectedly departed from her home for an extended stay far to the south. When she returned, the growing within the womb was pushing outward, expanding now to swell the mother's belly. It is not a secret that can be hidden for long.

This was not a society like our own where immorality is not only tolerated but often openly flaunted. Modesty and virtue were deeply ingrained into the fiber of the nation and was especially strong in the small towns and villages of Israel. Imagine the effect on that tiny village when Mary returned and the first of the village women began to notice the change in her.

Anyone who has ever lived in the tightly knit, closely bonded society of a small town or village can predict with some accuracy what happened next. At first there would have been only questioning looks and quick shaking of the heads. Surely such could not be so. Not Mary. Perhaps she was just putting on a little weight. And then more and more voices would have questioned, not openly, of course, but in whispers, at the well each day as they came together for water, or while doing the laundry on the banks of a stream.

Was Mary allowed to tell others of her visit from Gabriel? Matthew's comment, "she was *found* with child," would imply not. But even so, would such a "wildly fantastic" claim have quelled the rumors? A virgin birth? Mother of the Messiah? A child fathered by God Himself? Either she was mad or took them for absolute fools to imagine they would believe such a story. Now her departure from the village "in haste" took on new and ominous significance. (See Luke 1:39.) And poor Joseph. Victim of such infidelity. What would he do now?

"Then Joseph her husband, being a just man, and not willing to make her a publick example, was minded to put her away privily. But while he thought on these things, behold, the angel of the Lord appeared unto him in a dream, saying, Joseph, thou son of David, fear not to take unto thee Mary thy wife. . . .Then Joseph being raised from sleep did as the angel of the Lord had bidden him, and took unto him his wife." (Matthew 1:19-20, 24.)

Neither Luke nor Matthew gives us much detail, but we can read the pain and embarrassment between the lines. Here was a good man, faithful in every respect. What pain must have filled his soul to learn that his betrothed was with child! How could it be? Surely not Mary, not his lovely and chaste Mary. We can only guess at the agony of spirit he must have experienced at the confirmation of her "unfaithfulness."

How many men would let the bitterness and anger of such betrayal fester and boil over into the blind desire for revenge that causes one to strike out, seeking to hurt as deeply as you yourself are hurt? By Mosaic law, adultery was still punishable by death. (See, for example, John 8:5; Leviticus 20:10.) He could have taken her to the elders of the village and demanded justice. But, in spite of the pain he must have felt, in spite of the personal humiliation, he would not put his beloved Mary through the shame and danger of a public trial. He would simply dissolve the marriage contract quietly.

And then again, in one blinding instant of revelation, all was explained and put right. In response to the incredible announcement by Gabriel, Mary had simply said, "Behold the handmaid of the Lord." Now Joseph heard the same stunning pronouncement. We gain a glimpse of the greatness of the man from his response. Matthew says it in one phrase. "Then Joseph *being raised from sleep. . .* took unto him his wife." (Matthew 1:24.)

Again, as with Mary, the fantastic nature of the declaration was accepted without question. There was no vacillation. Surely he knew his fellow villagers well enough to know that a hasty marriage in the middle of the night would only fuel the rumors. All he would accomplish by such an action would be to bring the onus of doubt and shame upon himself. But the angel had spoken. His doubts were resolved. His Mary had been proven faithful. And so he arose from his bed and took her to be his wife.

"And it came to pass in those days, that there went out a decree from Caesar Augustus, that all the world should be taxed. . . . And all went to be taxed, every one into his own city. And Joseph also went up from Galilee, out of the city of Nazareth, unto Judaea, unto the city of David, which is called Bethlehem; (because he was of the house and lineage of David:) To be taxed with Mary his espoused wife, being great with child."

(Luke 2:1, 3-5.)

Bethlehem. The city of David. Ancient homeland of Israel's greatest king. In Hebrew it is called *Beth Lechem.* Literally, *Beth Lechem* means "The House of Bread."[8] How perfect that He who was to take the throne of David and become Israel's ultimate king should come to earth in the city of His illustrious ancestor! How fitting that He who would be known as the "Bread of Life" should enter mortality in the tiny village called "The House of Bread." (See John 6:35.)

Though His birth is celebrated in December, latter-day revelation explains that it actually occurred in the spring. (See D&C 20:1; James E. Talmage, *Jesus the Christ,* Classics in Mormon Literature Edition, Deseret Book, 1982, p. 98.) It would have been late March or early April as Joseph moved southward with Mary at his side, heavy with the living treasure in her womb. Spring is a time of glorious beauty in Israel. The "latter rains" water the parched soil, and in gratitude the earth responds with an explosion of grass and wildflowers. New life springs from the old with the wildest abundance. What better season to welcome him who would be called the "Prince of Life"? (See Acts 3:15.)

"And so it was, that, while they were there, the days were accomplished that she should be delivered. And she brought forth her firstborn son, and wrapped him in swaddling clothes, and laid him in a manger; because there was no room for them in the inn." (Luke 2:6-7.)

No room in the inn. If, as we believe, it was April and not December, then it was very likely Passover season in Jerusalem. This could explain the reason Joseph took Mary on the rigorous, sixty-mile journey to Judea when she was in the final month of her pregnancy. The Roman "taxing" mentioned by Luke was more accurately a census or enrollment. Each family head had to register and give an accounting of their property so that taxes could be levied. But while there was considerable flexibility in timing allowed to meet this requirement, if it was Passover season, that would allow them to meet two responsibilities. The Mosaic Law required that every adult male bring his sacrifices before the Lord (i.e., to the temple) each year at Passover. (See Exodus 23:14-19.) So by choosing this time of year, Joseph could fulfill both requirements.

Today we can hardly conceive of the magnitude of this most important of all Jewish festivals. From all over the empire, Jews returned to their homeland at Passover. Though it is difficult to determine exactly how large Jerusalem was during this period, a fairly accurate guess would place the population between one and two hundred thousand. Josephus tells us that during Passover "innumerable multitudes came thither [to Jerusalem] out of the country."[9] In another place, he was even more specific. Because the Paschal lamb had to be totally consumed by the family in the ritual meal, tradition stated that no less than ten and no more than twenty could gather for each lamb sacrificed. (See Exodus 12:10.) Josephus tells us that during one Passover of his time

(about A.D. 70), 256,500 lambs were sacrificed.[10] Even using the more conservative figure of ten, that still means the population of Jerusalem at Passover had swollen by more than 1000 percent to the staggering number of nearly three million people.

The throngs must have been incredible, the facilities throughout the city taxed beyond belief. And with Bethlehem only six miles south of Jerusalem, no wonder there was no room at the inn. Luke probably could have said with equal accuracy, "There was no room anywhere."

Often in the art and literature surrounding the Christmas story, the unknown, unnamed innkeeper of the scriptural account is viewed as selfish and uncaring, an insensitive oaf unmoved by the plight of a woman heavy with child. This may make for interesting art and literature, but it is not justified by the scriptural record. In the first place, the "inns" of the Middle East were not quaint and homey little buildings with thatched roofs and latticed windows from which warm lamplight beckoned the weary traveler. The inns of the Holy Land were typically large, fortress-like buildings, built around a spacious open square. Called *khans* or *caravanserai*, they provided stopping places for the caravans of the ancient world. Just as modern hotels and motels must provide parking for automobiles, so did a *caravanserai* have to provide a place where the donkeys, camels, and other animals could be safely cared for. Inside the *khan*, which was usually of two-story construction, all the "rooms" faced the courtyard. There were not private rooms. They were typically arched, open antechambers facing out onto the square. Here the traveler could build a small fire or sleep within clear view of his animals and goods. "In these hostelries, bazaars and markets were held, animals killed and meat sold, also wine and cider; so that they were a much more public place of resort than might at first be imagined."[11]

Even if there had been room at the inn, a *caravanserai* was hardly the ideal place for a woman in labor. Perhaps the innkeeper, moved with compassion at Mary's plight and knowing of her need and desire for privacy, offered them his stable. Perhaps Joseph found the place on his own. The scriptures do not say. But one thing is very likely, and this contradicts another popular misconception. The birth likely did not take place in a wooden shed with pitched roof as is so commonly depicted in nativity scenes around the world.

In Bethlehem today stands the Church of the Nativity. Beneath the church is a large grotto or cave. In southern Judea, including the area around Bethlehem, limestone caves are common. Such caves provided natural shelter for the flocks and herds of ancient Israel. They were warm, safe from inclement weather, and could easily be blocked to keep the animals safe for the night. The tradition that this grotto was the stable of Luke's account is very old and accepted by many scholars. Presi-dent Harold B. Lee, then of the Council of the Twelve, visited this grotto in 1958 and confirmed that in his mind it was "a hallowed spot, . . . a sacred place."[12]

So there in the sheltered warmth of the cave, beneath the limestone hills of Bethlehem, He who was to become the Good Shepherd—not of the sheep that grazed the hills of Israel, but of the human flock—was born and cradled in a manger.

That seems almost beyond our comprehension. Here was Jesus—a member of the Godhead, the Firstborn of the Father, the Creator, Jehovah of the Old Testament—now leaving His divine and holy station; divesting Himself of all that glory and majesty and entering the body of a tiny infant; helpless, completely dependent on His mother and earthly father. And that He should not come to the finest of earthly palaces and be swaddled in purple and showered with jewels, but should come to a lowly stable. Little wonder that the angel should say to Nephi, "Behold the condescension of God!" (1 Nephi 11:26.)

"And there were in the same country shepherds abiding in the field, keeping watch over their flock by night. And, lo, the angel of the Lord came upon them, and the glory of the Lord shone round about them: and they were sore afraid. And the angel said unto them, Fear not: for, behold, I bring you good tidings of great joy, which shall be to all people. For unto you is born this day in the city of David a Saviour, which is Christ the Lord. And this shall be a sign

unto you; *Ye shall find the babe wrapped in swaddling clothes, lying in a manger.*" (Luke 2:8-12.)

One of these verses is frequently misquoted: "Keeping watch over their *flocks* by night." But a more careful reading shows that it was not *flocks*, plural, but *flock*, singular. One scholar explained the significance: "There was near Bethlehem, on the road to Jerusalem, a tower known as *Migdal Eder*, or *the watchtower of the flock*. Here was the station where shepherds watched the flocks destined for sacrifice in the temple. . . . It was a settled conviction among the Jews that the Messiah was to be born in Bethlehem, and equally that he was to be revealed from Migdal Eder. The beautiful significance of the revelation of the infant Christ to shepherds watching the flocks destined for sacrifice needs no comment."[13]

Sometimes, in translation, the power of the original language is considerably lessened. While the words, in English, of the angel to the shepherds are beautiful and significant, we miss much of the electrifying impact the original words must have had on those men of Judea. Let us just examine two or three of the phrases as we assume they were given in Aramaic to the shepherds that night.

"*In the city of David.*" We have already seen that the Jews expected Bethlehem to be the birthplace of the Messiah. This in part stemmed directly from the prophet Micah, who centuries before had specified the place. (See Micah 5:2.)

"*Is born a Savior.*" The word which meant "Savior" was *Yeshua*. In the Greek New Testament that name was transliterated into *Hee-ay-sous*, or in English, "Jesus." When the angel announced to Joseph that Mary would bear a son, note what he said: "Thou shalt call his name Jesus [*Yeshua*]: for he shall *save* his people from their sins." (Matthew 1:21, emphasis added.)

"*Which is Christ.*" Our English word *Christ* is derived directly from the Greek, *Christos*. It means "the anointed one."[14] *Christos* was a direct translation of the Hebrew word, *Messhiach*, which meant exactly the same thing—the anointed one. *Messhiach* is of course transliterated into English as "Messiah."

"*The Lord.*" The simple title, "Lord," is perhaps the most significant of all, yet we totally miss its importance in the translation. In the Old Testament the name of God was written with four Hebrew consonants: YHVH. Because they did not write vowels, there has been some debate as to its proper pronunciation. Modern scholars often write it as YAHVEH, but the King James translators wrote it as JEHOVAH. The Jews of ancient times, however, viewed the name as being so sacred that it should not be pronounced out loud. Whenever they found it written, they would substitute the Hebrew word *Adonai*, meaning the Lord. The translators who produced the King James Version of the Old Testament honored that tradition of the Jews, and where they found the name YHVH (with very few exceptions) they wrote in "Lord." However, *adonai* can also be used as a title of respect for men, such as in the phrase, "My lord, the king." To distinguish between the two uses, the translators wrote *Lord* in small capital letters if it represented the name of deity, and regular upper and lower case letters if used normally. (See, for example, 2 Samuel 15:21, where both uses are found in the same verse.) The declaration of the angel to the shepherds obviously used *Lord* or *Adonai* in reference to deity; literally it could be translated *Jehovah.*

Now we begin to sense the impact of the angel's words upon these shepherds. In essence, here is his pronouncement: "Unto you is born this day in the city prophesied to be the birthplace of the Messiah, *Yeshua* [or Jesus], the Savior, who is the Anointed One (the Messiah), and who is also Jehovah, the God of your fathers."

"And they came with haste, and found Mary, and Joseph, and the babe lying in a manger. And when they had seen it, they made known abroad the saying which was told them concerning this child. And all they that heard it wondered at those things which were told them by the shepherds. But Mary kept all these things, and pondered them in her heart." (Luke 2:16-19.)

Gerald N. Lund is the author of The Coming of the Lord, *as well as several adventure novels, among them* The Alliance, The Freedom Factor, Leverage Point, *and* One in Thine Hand.

Notes

1. Alfred Edersheim, *Sketches of Jewish Social Life in the Days of Christ,* Wm. B. Eerdmans Publishing Company, Grand Rapids, Michigan, 1979, p. 70.

2. *Smith's Historical Geography,* as cited in Merrill F. Unger, ed., *Unger's Bible Dictionary,* 3d ed., Moody Press, Chicago, 1966, p. 779.

3. Edersheim, p. 105.

4. Edersheim, pp. 143-44.

5. Robert Young, *Analytical Concordance to the Bible,* Wm. B. Eerdmans Publishing Co., Grand Rapids, Michigan, 1972, p. 647.

6. From D&C 20:1 we learn that the birth date of the Savior was April 6 (see also James E. Talmage, *Jesus the Christ,* Salt Lake City: The Church of Jesus Christ of Latter-day Saints, p. 98). Counting nine months backwards puts the time somewhere around August.

7. In Luke 2:24 we are told that Mary and Joseph offered as the required sacrifice for their firstborn son two turtledoves or pigeons. In Leviticus 12:6-8, where the requirement is given, we are told that it should be a lamb, but if the family "be not able," i.e., financially cannot afford a lamb, they may instead offer the turtledoves.

8. Unger, p. 40.

9. Josephus, *Antiquities,* XVII, ix, 3.

10. Josephus, *Wars of the Jews,* VI, ix, 3.

11. Unger, p. 527.

12. Harold B. Lee, "I Walked Today Where Jesus Walked," *BYU Speeches of the Year,* December 10, 1958, p. 5.

13. M.R. Vincent, *Word Studies in the New Testament,* MacDonald Publishing Company, Mac-Dill AFB, Florida, n.d., p. 142.

14. Unger, p. 195.

CHRISTMAS EVE IN FRONT OF THE OPEN OVEN DOOR

by Leonard J. Arrington

Picture an isolated, two-room, wooden frame home on a windy prairie in southern Idaho. Coyotes howl in the distance. Despite wintry weather, the sky is clear and the stars are brilliant. There is a faint trace in the sky of an aurora borealis, or what is commonly referred to as "northern lights." One can hear horses in a nearby corral breathing heavily and occasional sounds of late-night munching from two milk cows. Add to the picture a family, with a father and mother and three children—LeRoy, seven; Leonard, four; and Marie, two—sitting in front of an open oven door. Father, a hardy son of Tennessee mountaineers, is peeling an apple while telling about hunting raccoons and razorback wild hogs when he was a boy. Mother, humming faintly while her black-haired husband tells his stories, gets up to shake the skillet a few times while she makes popcorn. When it erupts, she distributes it to the eager family. Father likes to eat popcorn with sugar and cream, just as the Prophet Joseph Smith did.

It is a joyous moment, not untypical of every wintry night on that southern Idaho homestead in the early 1920s. But there is one difference—this is Christmas Eve and this is a Latter-day Saint family. On this first Christmas Eve that I remember, my father, Noah Arrington, is telling stories about Christmas in the Tennessee hill country. My red-headed mother, Edna Corn Arrington, reared in a Methodist home in Oklahoma, sings Christmas songs, recites poems she learned in school, and tells stories about Jesus—His birth, His teaching in the synagogue, His Sermon on the Mount, His healing of the sick of mind and body.

My image of an Idaho Christmas remained with me as I grew up and then went to college. It came forcibly to mind when I served in the U.S. Army in North Africa and Italy during World War II. The Christmases of 1943, 1944, 1945 were all spent overseas, and the loneliness of soldier life induced feelings of nostalgia. I resolved, in my own family, to try to duplicate the warm Christmas experiences of the Arringtons in southern Idaho.

Later my wife and I accepted a position at Utah State University in Logan,

Utah, and our three children—James, Carl, and Susan—were born and reared there.

From the time our children were small, we held a family devotional on Christmas Eve. The program began with a family prayer, followed by Christmas songs; then each member of the family presented some part of the program. One read a Christmas story, another played the piano, a third might have recited a poem or put on a skit. I read the Christmas story from Luke and gave a sermonette; Mother reminded us of an episode from a past Christmas.

As the children grew older, their contributions became more creative. James, now an actor-playwright, liked to write and perform playlets; Carl, a writer for *People* magazine, told original stories with a Christmas theme; Susan, a home-maker and author, enjoyed playing original compositions on the piano. And so on. Being a historian, I recounted interesting Christmas experiences of early Latter-day Saints—such as Joseph Smith skating on the ice with his son Frederick, Brigham Young driving to the mill to get grain to distribute to widows, Wilford Woodruff devoting the entire day to shucking corn, and Heber J. Grant spending most of the day signing books to be sent out to bishops around the Church. We closed our devotional with family prayer.

When the little children were put to bed, the older ones then gathered together for our annual "family meeting." I made the financial report of the family's "condition of affairs." How close were we toward paying off the mortgage? Have we made out a will—just in case? Is there any heavy debt hanging over us? How is our job and what are the future prospects? Everyone was encouraged to ask questions.

Each person was then asked to list, on paper provided for the purpose, five resolutions for the forthcoming year. These were read out loud. Having committed ourselves, we suggested resolutions for each other. For example, there might have been a resolution that one of us take a shower more often, another should please show up for dinner on time. Other resolutions: grow a mustache, quit getting jittery over winter driving, quit snoring, stop going out with "that creep." Sometimes this was done in good humor, as for instance the year my little girl resolved that I should take her, and her alone, out to dinner once a month. I managed to do it nine times during the year that followed, and was asked to do the same thing the next year by every other member of the family.

We reversed the custom of making resolutions for each other one year and decided to write down something nice about each of those present. After these were read, with many nods of approval, the slips were given to the person for whom they were written. Thus, I learned that my family didn't regard me as a penny pincher, appreciated that I was always in a good mood, and liked my taste for women (their mother).

One year we made predictions for

the coming year, not only events nationally and internationally, but what would happen in the family. Susan went out on a limb to predict a major earthquake in Chile. As we read these over the next year, we were astounded that there had, indeed, been an earthquake in Chile that had killed two thousand people. She became our prophetess. As to family predictions, my son-in-law, whose home is in a mountainous area having frequent visits from deer and elk looking for winter fodder, was told that he would suffer asphyxiation from elk breath. Another predicted she would have a baby in August, a way of announcing to us her pregnancy. Still another predicted they would be forced to commit their parakeet to the state mental hospital.

One year the chairman (we rotate each year) asked each person to bring a favorite poem to read or recite. One read Wordsworth's "Lines Written in Early Spring"; another, "If" by Rudyard Kipling; a third, "Choose Something Like a Star" from Robert Frost; a fourth, Kasantzakis's rendition of "The Odyssey"; a fifth, Dylan Thomas's "Do Not Go Gentle Into That Good Night"; a sixth, a Shakespearean sonnet; and another, Robert Frost's "One Step Backward Taken."

The next year we were requested to bring a favorite record to play. The amazing variety showed the differences in individual tastes that ranged from Beethoven to the Beach Boys, from Maria Callas to Madonna.

The historian in me knew that if I

kept a proper file, some personal information would be valuable to those writing personal and family histories in the future. So there were always some "fun" questions and some "thought" and self-revelatory questions that each had to answer on paper, date and sign, and, after reading to the group, turn over to me for the family archives. The following are examples of questions:

Question: What are some things you most enjoy? Answers: bubbling brooks, snow-covered mountains, birds in the wild, people who make sacrifices for others, "La Boheme," the sound of the organ in our chapel, mother's pies.

Question: If you could turn into an animal, which would you most enjoy being? Answers: a sleek cat that stubbornly retains her independence, a tiger that escapes from his cage and livens up a city street, a horse that carries on his back a whole neighborhood of children on Saturday afternoon, a hen that proudly cackles after it has laid an egg, a kangaroo because it can jump away from any difficulty.

Question: What do you consider the best personality or character traits a person can have? Answers: sensitivity to others' needs, being able to make people feel good, teachability, having a sense of humor, being insightful without being pompous.

Question: What living person do you most admire, family members excepted, and why? Some responses over the years: David O. McKay, Spencer W. Kimball, John F. Kennedy, Winston Churchill, Mother Teresa, Margaret Thatcher,

Belle Spafford, Lowell Bennion.

Question: What was the most terrifying experience you ever had? One told of a ride in a jeep over rough country terrain; another told of being introduced to an audience and not being able to speak; one told of rappelling up a mountain and walking over the edge of a cliff; another told of a dream in which he was sitting on a hill and his parents walked away and left him; another told of walking down a ghetto street with two suitcases, fearful every minute that he would be mugged. A grandmother told of the time her mother told her that the buzzards would get her if she didn't wear a hat. Once she went outside and forgot to wear her hat. When she saw buzzards circling overhead, she became so terrified that she couldn't even run back into the house. She just sat down and screamed.

Other questions: Assuming you are converted to the gospel of Jesus Christ, what was the single most important experience or idea that converted you? What, if anything, has been an obstacle to your complete and continuous conversion? What was the most spiritual experience you ever had? What book, aside from the Bible and Book of Mormon, has influenced you most?

As each person read his/her answer to the question of the evening, there was always lively discussion and the sharing of thoughts. We felt a very intimate family spirit. And, because it was Christmas Eve, the spirit of Christ came into our midst. It was like sitting around the open oven door.

When members of the household were on LDS missions, they were asked to prepare something to be read at the meeting. If there was an illness, there was always a family prayer offered in behalf of the afflicted.

With such Christmas Eve festivities, our family has been able to keep alive a tradition of closeness and mutual understanding that existed on a lonely Idaho homestead many years ago. With grandchildren and great-grandchildren, the tradition is the highlight of the Christmas season. And this particular grandpa, like his father, continues to eat his popcorn with sugar and cream.

Leonard J. Arrington has published widely throughout his distinguished career. He is the author (or coauthor) of, among others: Mothers of the Prophets, Presidents of the Church, From Quaker to Latter-day Saint, Building the City of God, Brigham Young: American Moses, The Mormon Experience: A History of the Latter-day Saints, *and* Great Basin Kingdom.

AARON'S CHRISTMAS TREE

by Alma J. Yates

It was my very first Christmas after Dad died. I was only seven then, but I was the man of the house—at least that's what Dad had always told me whenever he went somewhere. Whenever he had to go away, he'd say to me, "Son, you're the man of the house while I'm gone, and I want you to look after Mom and Aaron."

Aaron's my little brother, and he was only four that Christmas. We didn't have much money with Dad gone; at least that's what Mom told me. Now when she went to the store she didn't buy peanuts and candy like she used to when Dad was still alive. Aaron didn't get much for his birthday either—just a ball, and it wasn't even new. I didn't tell Aaron because he liked the ball just fine.

Christmas was getting close, and I was getting excited. I told Aaron all about Christmas. He couldn't remember the other ones because he was just a baby then. I told him about the lights and the decorations, and about Jesus in the manger, and about the presents and the stockings and Santa Claus. Aaron doesn't talk much, but he listens a lot. I really like Aaron because he's a good listener.

Lots of times when we were in bed at night, Aaron would ask me to tell him about Christmas. I'd talk and talk until I was sure he was asleep, but as soon as I stopped talking he'd whisper, "Alma, tell me again," and I'd have to start all over. He'd never go to sleep until I finally told him that my throat was sore and that I had to stop talking.

The thing Aaron liked to hear about most was the Christmas tree. Whenever I talked about the tree, his eyes got really big and he'd smile. He always asked me if we would have a tree, and I'd say, "Sure. Everybody has a tree. You can't have Christmas without a tree." Well, I shouldn't have said that, because later Mom told me we couldn't afford to have a tree.

I was in trouble then, because it was getting close to Christmas and everybody on our street had trees in their windows. Aaron was getting more excited. He asked me every night to tell him about Christmas and the Christmas tree.

I didn't know what to do, but I knew

45

I had to do something. Then on Sunday my Primary teacher told a story about a pioneer boy who found his own Christmas tree. He just went outside and found a tree in the woods and cut it down. It didn't cost him anything. I didn't hear the rest of the story. All I could think about was getting a tree.

On the way home I looked for a tree. We weren't pioneers or anything like that; we were just poor. We didn't live in the woods, either; but there were some Christmas trees growing in our neighborhood. Lots of people grew Christmas trees in their yards, and there were some growing in the park, but most of them were too big for our house. We didn't have a very big house, so I knew I had to get a little tree that would fit.

I looked and looked, and I almost decided there weren't any trees our size when I saw one in Brother Hubbard's yard, right next to the sidewalk. The tree was about as high as my mom, and it was really fluffy with lots of bluish-green branches. That was the tree I was going to get for Aaron.

That night in bed I told Aaron all about the tree and asked him if he would help me cut it down. He said he would, and then he asked me to tell him about Christmas again.

The next day, when Mom was in the

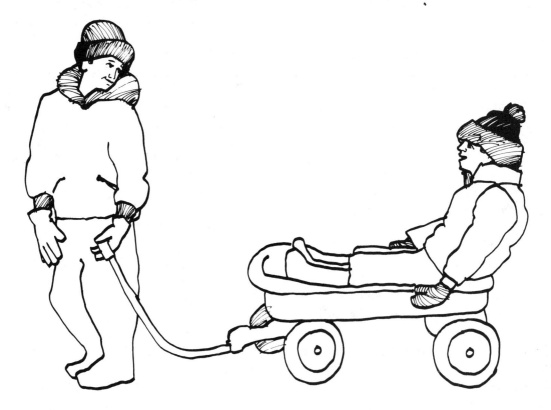

46

house cooking supper, Aaron and I went to the garage and got an axe and one of Dad's saws. We put the axe and the saw into my wagon and started down the street. At first Aaron pushed while I pulled, but after a while he climbed into the wagon and rode.

Brother and Sister Hubbard weren't home when we got to their house. I was glad because I didn't want to ask them if I could cut down their tree. I figured it would be easier to just cut it down like the boy in the story and not ask anybody anything. Besides, I didn't think Brother Hubbard would mind. He was the nicest man I knew, next to my dad. Brother Hubbard was our home teacher, and he visited us all the time. He did lots of nice things for us, especially after Dad died. He told us that whatever we needed he'd try to get for us. So I didn't think he'd care if we cut down his tree, because Aaron really needed a Christmas tree and I didn't know how else to get him one.

I got right to work, but Aaron just sat in the wagon and watched. Although he was cold, he didn't ask to go home. He wanted a Christmas tree. First I had to saw off some of the branches so I could chop at the trunk. That was kind of hard because the branches prickled my hands and face.

As soon as I got the branches out of the way, I got the axe out of the wagon and started to chop, but it didn't work very well. The axe was too big. It kept hitting into the branches and bouncing off the trunk. I knocked some bark off, but I couldn't chop down the tree. I

kept trying, though, until I dropped the axe on my foot. Then I just had to cry because my foot really hurt. I didn't let Aaron see me, though. I put my head down close to the trunk and pretended I was looking at it.

I finally decided to use the saw, and it worked better. Pretty soon I had cut halfway through the trunk. But the tree still didn't fall over, and the saw kept getting stuck. It would squeak and then stop. I pushed and pulled and kicked the tree, but that just hurt my foot. I was tired by then, and my hands and feet were cold. I started to cry. This time Aaron saw me, and he started to cry, too. When I tried to get him to stop crying, he said he was cold and wanted to go home and that we could get Mom to come back and help us.

While we were both crying, Brother and Sister Hubbard drove up in their car. At first, they didn't know what we were doing; but as soon as they got out of their car, they could see. Brother Hubbard's a nice man. He's old—kind of like a grandpa—and he's my best friend next to Aaron.

"What are you boys doing, Alma?" he asked when he walked over to us. Sister Hubbard stayed by the car and watched. I wasn't crying anymore. I just stared at Brother Hubbard's big feet. They were bigger than Dad's. Aaron stopped crying, too.

"We're cutting a Christmas tree for Christmas," Aaron said. "We're going to put it in our house. Do you want to help us?"

Brother Hubbard didn't say anything,

and I didn't dare look at him. "We can't buy one," I whispered, "because we don't have any money. But my Primary teacher told me about a pioneer boy who cut down a tree, and he didn't have to buy it. We aren't pioneers like the boy in the story, but we thought it would be all right, since we didn't have a tree. Yours was the very best tree. I hope you don't need it."

Brother Hubbard thought for a minute and then asked, "Does your mother know you're here, Alma?" He put his hand on my shoulder, and I shook my head.

"I'm the man of the house," I said, "and I wanted to surprise her." I looked up at Brother Hubbard and then at Aaron and then back at Brother Hubbard. "Can I talk to you for a minute?" I pulled Brother Hubbard by the hand and took him behind the tree so Aaron couldn't hear us. "I've been telling Aaron all about Christmas, but now it doesn't look like we'll have too much Christmas. My friend Tommy says Santa Claus is just your mom and dad. Well, we don't have a dad now, and Mom is poor, so if there isn't a Santa Claus, we won't have any Christmas at all unless we get a tree. That's why I needed a tree. I really want Aaron to have a Christmas. He can't remember the other ones, and I want him to have a real good Christmas, even if Santa Claus doesn't come."

I don't know why I started to bawl. I guess my foot still hurt. Brother Hubbard patted my shoulder and said, "Well, Alma, it doesn't look like that

tree will be doing much good where it is now. Do you want me to help you finish cutting it down?"

I looked up at him, and he was smiling, so I figured everything was okay.

"Alma, don't worry too much about what your friend Tommy said. I don't have a dad or mom anymore, but Santa visits me every Christmas."

"He does?"

"Sure. And I bet he'll come to your house. In fact, I know he will."

Brother Hubbard dragged the tree home for us, and I pulled Aaron in the wagon. When Mom saw the tree, she was really happy. She even cried.

On Christmas Eve, Aaron and Mom and I sat around the Christmas tree and sang. Mom told us about Jesus and all the people who came to see Him when He was born. We were almost ready for bed when someone knocked on our door. I answered it, and there stood Brother Hubbard with a big box in his arms. It was filled with oranges and apples and nuts and fruitcake and a turkey and candy and lots of other good things. Mom invited Brother Hubbard in, and while Aaron and I looked through the box, she and Brother Hubbard whispered in the corner. When they were through, Brother Hubbard put his arms around me and Aaron and asked us if we were ready for Santa Claus. I nodded my head, but I really didn't believe Santa would come. I was afraid Tommy was right and that Brother Hubbard was just trying to make me feel good.

I guess Brother Hubbard knew what I

was thinking, because he patted me on the back and smiled, "He'll be here, Alma. You wait and see. He hasn't forgotten you and Aaron."

Aaron and I had to go to bed then. I was tired and wanted to go to sleep, but Aaron wouldn't let me. He made me tell him everything I knew about Christmas. I don't know which one of us fell asleep first, but it didn't seem like I'd been sleeping very long when I felt Aaron shaking me and heard him whisper, "Alma, he's here! He's here! Wake up!"

Finally I opened my eyes. I couldn't see anything but a crack of light under our bedroom door. Someone had left the light on in the living room. "Who's here?" I asked grumpily.

"Santa Claus!"

"Santa Claus? Who said?"

"I can hear him, Alma. I can hear him. He's out by the Christmas tree!"

"Go back to bed, Aaron. I'll turn the light off. It's not Santa Claus. Just go back to bed."

I stumbled down the hall to the living room. Aaron was right behind me. I was too tired to stop him. All I wanted to do was turn the light off and get back into bed. But before I could, Aaron yelled, "It *is* Santa Claus! Alma, it *is* Santa Claus!"

I turned around and there he was! Aaron ran and kissed him on his white beard. I couldn't even move. All I could do was stare. Santa's eyes got big. He was surprised. I was afraid he was

going to go away and not leave us anything. Mom used to say that if we didn't go to sleep, Santa wouldn't come.

"Aaron, come here," I hissed. "We aren't supposed to be here." But Aaron didn't listen to me. Santa was holding him, and Aaron was squeezing his neck and wouldn't let go.

All of a sudden, Santa started to laugh. He sounded a little like Brother Hubbard, but Brother Hubbard is skinny, not fat. He put Aaron and me on his knees and laughed and hugged us. He looked at me and said, "I heard you didn't think I was going to come." I looked at the floor. "Well, I'm here," he said. "I brought you and Aaron something very special, but you must go back to bed while I work. You'll see everything in the morning."

Santa carried us to our beds and tucked us in. He kissed us both on the forehead, and his beard tickled my cheeks and nose. It felt good. I didn't go to sleep for a long time. I listened to Santa doing things in the living room. When he left, I listened for him on the roof, but I didn't hear anything.

I wanted to go out and see what he'd brought, but I didn't dare. I knew I had to go to sleep. As I lay there thinking, I was glad that I was the man of the house and that Brother Hubbard and I could get Aaron a Christmas tree.

Alma J. Yates has written several novels, including Horse Thieves, The Miracle of Miss Willie, *and* The Inner Storm. *"Aaron's Christmas Tree" was first published in the* Friend, *December 1982.*

THE JOY
OF CHRISTMAS

by Dell Van Orden

It was 1947, and I could hardly wait for Christmas. I had just turned twelve and was now a Boy Scout, something I had longed for ever since my older brother became a Scout nearly two years earlier. I wanted to become an Eagle more than just about anything in life. But I didn't intend to stop there. I wanted to earn every merit badge available.

President George Albert Smith had visited our town in Idaho earlier that year and spoken at a Scout banquet, to which my dad took my brother and me. Seeing the President of the Church in his Scout uniform only intensified my feeling that if I were to become the very best Scout possible, I, too, would have to be properly outfitted in a fine Boy Scout uniform.

I pored over the pages of *Boy's Life* magazine, looking at the advertisements. I dreamed of having my own shiny new cooking kit and canteen—not surplus World War II items that so many Scouts in my troop had, but the new accessories I saw advertised.

As the Christmas season approached, I let the word out to my family that I didn't want any kids' stuff—no games or toys. I just wanted items to make me a better-equipped Boy Scout. After we put up and decorated the Christmas tree and placed the presents underneath, I could hardly contain myself.

One package, with my name on it, was particularly exciting. The wrapping paper, however, wasn't very pretty. It was all wrinkled because it had been used several times before. We had been taught during the war to not throw away anything, and so we saved our wrapping paper, along with the ribbons and used name tags, from year to year. It was always a challenge to find in the Christmas box a tag from a previous year with the right names "to" and "from" already written on it.

But that year the outside wrapping didn't matter. I had run my fingers across the package many times, and I could tell from the shape that it was a hunting knife in a scabbard. I just knew the knife would be "Official Boy Scout." My excitement was almost more than I could bear.

The Friday before Christmas I received a telephone call. It was from my

Scoutmaster. He said that our troop had been asked by the Salvation Army to help deliver Christmas baskets the next day to the poor and the elderly, and he asked if I would help. More from not knowing how to say "no" to my Scoutmaster than from any desire to help, I mumbled that I would.

Saturday dawned cold and blustery. The snow was whipped about by a strong wind common on the Idaho flatlands. "Why?" I asked myself a hundred times. "Why did I ever agree to help deliver those Christmas baskets?"

As I walked to the Salvation Army building about a mile from home, the wind-driven snow knifed at my face, causing tears to flow from my eyes and freezing on my cheeks. With each step, I grew more reluctant to want to help — a feeling that was greatly magnified when I got to the Salvation Army and found that only a few Scouts had showed up. I was cold. I wanted to go home.

But something happened that day that still burns brightly in my heart.

With each passing home, as I was greeted at the door by an elderly or poor person, I could feel, almost tangibly, the joy and appreciation that those Christmas baskets brought. Widows hugged and thanked me for what I was doing. When they realized that somebody cared, that they were not forgotten at Christmastime, they cried.

Inwardly, I cried, too.

I realized, probably for the first time in my life, the joy of helping to lift the burdens of others. Delivering baskets to the poor and aged at Christmastime was what the spirit of Christmas was all about. It wasn't the gifts underneath the tree at home; it was the joy of Christlike service.

I forgot about the cold. I forgot about wanting to go home. I just wanted to hurry to the next house and feel the joy that I knew would come as I delivered the basket of food and goodies. It was a happiness I hadn't really experienced before, and I didn't want to lose the feeling.

Yes, there was a hunting knife under the tree that Christmas, and later there would come the shiny new Boy Scout cooking kit and canteen. We even quit reusing wrapping paper and tags. But there was never another Christmas quite like that one more than forty years ago.

It was the first Christmas that I really found Christ.

Dell Van Orden is the editor of the Church News.

THE OLD WREATH

by Lowell M. Durham, Jr.

The wreath had come that brittle cold winter,
From a widow and child Father had helped when
He'd taken them a cord of good pitch wood
And stacked it neatly in the snow.

All bundled up, the young daughter, Martha,
Handed Father the fragile Christmas wreath
Made from willows and an old worn ribbon—
A red ribbon we had seen in her hair.

Now every year since, the wreath had hung
Proudly at Christmas on the front door.
And each year I watch Father hang the wreath
And see a certain reverence in the task.

This year a three-foot grandson scowled and asked,
"Grandpa, why do you hang up that old wreath?"
Father paused, then said quietly, "For Martha,
And because—it's the real meaning of Christmas."

THE SIFTING

by Lowell M. Durham, Jr.

December starts the sifting
Through old orange boxes carefully packed
By hands wanting to save the traditions
From little hands that don't know the ritual.

Mother's windless winnowing through layers
Of lights and gold, stars and clothespin soldiers,
Is a sifting that renews remembrances of Christmas
Like a quiet accumulation of new snow.

She finds it there—in a safely protected corner,
A box in the box, a treasure swaddled in tissue,
Grandmother's ancient ornament glowing with visions
Of all the Christmas times that were.

And now, held like an eggshell by hands too young,
The warm angularities of light teach again
The wonder of this new Christmas
And of all the Christmas times that ever were.

*Lowell M. Durham, Jr., formerly the president and
general manager of Deseret Book, is president of
ZCMI. His poetry has been published in the Church
magazines, and he wrote the lyrics to the hymn, ''As
the Shadows Fall.''*

THE NIGHT AFTER CHRISTMAS

by Kris Mackay

'Twas the night *after* Christmas. Again through the house,
No one stirred. Not a soul. No, not even that mouse.
The town clock was striking a quarter past one
And we were bedraggled, festivities done.

We'd partied that year and then partied some more,
Till the part of our brains that planned parties was sore.
But, oh! Oh, what parties! Ours ranked with the best.
So we were convinced we had earned a good rest.

I turned out the lights and then put out the cat;
I tucked in the children, gave each one a pat;
I straightened their covers and blew them a kiss;
But then, without warning, sensed something amiss.

I stepped to the parlor, I paused at the door,
And peered through the gloom at toys strewn on the floor.
A teddy bear leaned half askew from a shelf.
I felt strangely dejected, in spite of myself.

We'd straightened the corners, swept most of the muss,
Had tried to coax order back out of the fuss.
But wrappings we'd labored on—filled with such love—
Lay empty and torn as an old, worn-out glove.

A stray piece of tinsel peeped out from one sack's
Original contents of ball and some jacks.
Our stockings still hung from the chimney, it's true,
But not round and plump. They'd been stretched black and blue.

54

Grandpa's hung limply, bulged out and all baggy,
And Grandma's, poor thing, appeared equally saggy
As if they'd been put through some war or a riot.
They hung there so downcast, sad, droopy, and quiet.

I stood at the living room door. It was chilly.
And now when I looked at the room, it looked silly.
Where was excitement, or glitter, or fun
Now that the sugarplum dreaming was done?

The tree wasn't fresh as it had been before;
I winced when three needles fell *Plunk!* to the floor.
I plugged in its lights, plugged them into the wall,
And tried to recapture some thrill from it all.

But the squeals and the "oohs" and the "aahs" of the day
Had all vanished. No trace. They'd just faded away.
I stood there alone in the dark and the cold,
And right at that moment I felt very old.

I stood all alone, and no longer felt jolly.
Then I shook myself—hard—and I muttered, "By golly,
You're acting so strangely, so much like a dope!
Surely somewhere tonight there is still joy and hope."

Away to the window I flew, for a start,
To search for some *something* to lighten my heart.
I reached for the stars, for stars strong and able.
And yes! They still shone! Like the one o'er a stable.

They hung there the same as I'd seen them last night,
So shining and solid, so warm and so bright.
And suddenly the shambles we'd made of this room
Retreated, and joy and sweet peace filled the gloom.

The wonder of Christmas was not gone at all.
It was there in our hearts. And a voice, still and small,
Whispered, "Peace and good cheer. I have conquered the world,
Not for one night alone, but my star was unfurled

For forever. Oh please, have a most merry season,
But don't let the tinsel push out the real reason
You celebrate Christmas. Be happy, and play.
But *remember:* I came to bring life on that day."

I turned out the lights, but the glow that I felt
Went with me to bed. It never did melt.
I snuggled in softly, as cozy as toast,
And I chuckled inside, knowing what matters most.

Oh, Santa's important, his presents are nice.
But true Christmas joy (if you'll take my advice)
Comes from Christ and His loving—a gift that will last,
After all of the tinsel and glitter are past.

I yawned and I smiled. As I drifted to sleep
I knew I'd been offered one gift I could keep.
If I treasured my gift for days three-sixty-five,
The spirit of Christmas would live on, and thrive.

No need for a letdown when wrappings are torn.
The real gift was given the night *He* was born.

Kris Mackay has been published in The Reader's
Digest *and* Parade *magazines, and has written
the books* No Greater Love, In Loving Hands, *and*
The Outstretched Arms.

A CHRISTMAS NEEDLEPOINT

by Brent A. Barlow

During the early part of December 1970 I was asked to speak in one of our church meetings during the Christmas season. At that time Susan and I, with our two small children, were living in Tallahassee, Florida, where I was working on a graduate degree at Florida State University.

In my talk I related a story contained in a book written by Lloyd C. Douglas and published in 1933 entitled *Precious Jeopardy, A Christmas Story.*

The story is about a man named Phil Garland, his wife, Shirley, and their two children, Polly and Junior. Phil was very disgruntled as he was driving home on Christmas Eve. He had just lost his job.

When he arrived home, Shirley greeted him in her usual pleasant manner. But she, too, became discouraged as Phil conveyed the job loss to her. Their financial situation had been difficult enough when Phil was working. He now seemed even more distant to Shirley and the children than he had during the past few months.

That evening Shirley tried to include Phil in some of the Christmas Eve activities with Polly and Junior. But Phil just grumbled at the price of the gifts. He reminded Shirley that in their tight financial condition they couldn't afford any gifts at all. He said Christmas was overly commercialized anyway. Eventually, Shirley helped Polly and Junior get ready for bed. Then, tearfully, she retired to their bedroom.

A few minutes later she heard Phil calling from the hallway. He yelled for her to get the pliers. "I've stepped on a needle," he groaned.

Shirley brought the pliers, and Phil used them to tug on the needle protruding from his foot. Out came half of the needle. "That means," he muttered, "the other half of it is still in my foot." He and Shirley discussed the possibility of going to the hospital that night to have the other half removed. But Phil assured her it could wait until morning.

The next day, Christmas, Phil drove toward the hospital but then paused outside. Somewhere he had heard that if you get a tiny piece of metal in your body and do not remove it, it can eventually move to one of the vital organs and cause death. For some reason Phil decided to leave the other half of the needle in his foot and take the eventual consequences, if and when they occurred. He drove home and told Shirley that everything had been taken care of.

From that moment Phil believed his life was in jeopardy. He really didn't know if he was going to live from one day to the next. He decided he would try and make the most of life on a day-to-day basis. There was a marked change in him. He treated Shirley with more kindness and spent time playing with Polly and Junior. Phil had a very pleasant Christmas Day with his family. He didn't know, after all, if he would be alive tomorrow.

Tomorrow came and Phil Garland found himself alive. For the second day in a row he was extra considerate to his wife and children because it might be the last day of his life. The story proceeded with examples of Phil spending more time with Shirley, Polly, and Junior on a day-by-day basis. He also took daily odd jobs in the community to financially support his family.

Precious Jeopardy ended, as it began, on Christmas Eve, one year later. It was in sharp contrast to the previous Christmas because Phil was so happy.

On Christmas Eve, Phil played a few games and romped with the children. Before putting them to bed they exchanged a few small gifts they had made during the year. During those months Phil had made a walnut sewing cabinet for Shirley. He took her to his work area and presented his gift to her. Shirley was again tearful, but this year

it was because of Phil's thoughtfulness.

As the clock struck midnight Shirley informed Phil that she also had a gift for him. She handed Phil a small box which he opened. There was a tiny fragment of steel pierced through red velvet. It was the other half of the needle Phil *thought* was in his foot. The story ends:

"You'll forgive me—won't you dear," Shirley begged. "It was just the next day—I was moving the rug and found the other half of the needle. I wanted to tell you—at once.

"But you see," Shirley went on, brokenly, "this other half of the needle gave you back to us. I couldn't risk losing you again, could I? And it made you so brave and kind!"

Phil's arm tightened around her shoulders, protectively. He slowly released a long pent-up sigh that sounded as if he might have come a great distance. "Well, thanks, Shirley," he stammered. "I'm glad to have it. Just what I wanted. No, no, don't cry, darling. It's Christmas."

After graduating from Florida State University during the summer of 1971 we moved to Carbondale, Illinois, where I accepted a teaching position at Southern Illinois University. As the Christmas season approached at the end of the year, I went to the university library, checked out *Precious Jeopardy*, and again reread the dramatic Christmas story.

My appreciation increased for Lloyd Douglas and his story, but a few months later I had an unusual experience which brought the message even more vividly to mind.

It was Saturday, March 4, 1972. I had awakened about 5:00 A.M. to grade student papers. Unknown to me, Susan had been sewing a dress for our daughter, Tammy. Evidently Tammy had taken her new dress down the hall to hold it up before her in the mirror. She had unintentionally dropped a needle on the carpet floor in the process.

As I reached the end of the hall during that early morning hour, I felt a dull, yet sensational pain in my left foot. The pain was so intense I dropped to the floor and grabbed my foot. To my alarm I found I had stepped on the needle. I called for help. Susan and the children rushed from their bedrooms and gathered around me as I sat wincing with pain and holding my foot.

The whole event was too coincidental. Somehow this all seemed painfully familiar. Susan got the pliers and I pulled on the needle. It wouldn't come out. We agreed that I should go immediately to Doctor's Memorial Hospital a mile or so from our house. I found I could drive our station wagon even though I had a needle in my foot. Unlike Phil Garland in *Precious Jeopardy,* however, there was no question as to whether the needle should stay in or come out.

It was about 6:00 A.M. as I limped into the emergency room and told the nurse on duty what had happened. She took me to an operating room and notified one of the physicians.

The doctor arrived a few minutes later and did a preliminary examination. The needle was so deeply imbedded in my foot that he had to call a surgeon to remove it.

The physician on duty instructed me to rest on the operating table until the surgeon arrived. "This is not a real emergency, Mr. Barlow," he said. "Not to you, it's not," I replied. He then left. There I was, waiting, on the operating table for nearly forty-five minutes.

During that time I did some serious thinking about things that seem to matter most when one believes his life to be in peril. I immediately recalled my Christmas talk in Tallahassee just a year previous. What irony! I was living Phil Garland's experience. I thought about life—not only about dying, but more importantly, about living. Life is indeed precious, and I had often been complacent. I had taken for granted so many things, including my children and my wife.

The surgeon finally arrived and began his examination of the needle in my foot. I asked, "Is it true that a tiny piece of metal in the body can eventually cause you to die if it is not removed?" The doctor smiled. "I think I've heard that before, but I am not certain it is true." He continued the examination and then continued, "You won't have to worry," he assured me, "yours will be out in just a few minutes."

The surgeon gave me a local anesthetic, so I was conscious during the operation. I continued to think on the incident and couldn't help but be a little philosophical about the experience.

While lying on the operating table, I continued to reflect on life. Symbolically, I realized, we all have a tiny piece of metal in our bodies. It is called mortality. It was at that moment that I fully realized for the first time in my life that I, too, would eventually die.

After the surgery I returned home and shared some of my thoughts with Susan. She meant more to me than she ever had before. And so did our children.

During that day and those that followed I began thinking more seriously about life. On long walks I thought about life after death. But I thought even more intently about life before death. What was the purpose of this life? What things mattered most? What were my priorities? Where did I spend most of my time?

My foot eventually healed, but the vivid impression of the experience has never left me. Several thoughts have helped me arrive at a philosophy, not so much about dying, but more importantly about living. Two thoughts have been particularly helpful.

One is by Henry David Thoreau. He went to the woods surrounding Walden Pond, he said, "because I wished to live deliberately, to confront only the essential facts of life, and see if I could not learn what it had to teach, and not, when I came to die, discover that I had not lived. I did not wish to live what was not life, living is so dear." (*Masters of American Literature,* Houghton Mifflin, 1959, p. 405.)

The other thought is by Albert Schweitzer. He wrote, "The tragedy of man is not that man dies but what dies within man while he is alive." (*Vital Quotations,* Bookcraft, 1968, p. 216.)

And still other thoughts come during the Christmas season. Because of my experience with *Precious Jeopardy,* Christmas has taken on renewed meaning to me. The Savior's birth, life, death, and resurrection all have become more meaningful. I am beginning to realize the significance of His statement when He said, "I am come that they might have life, and that they might have it more abundantly." (John 10:10.) Certainly part of that abundance is experience with our loved ones, our parents, brothers and sisters, friends, children, and husband or wife. And the entire Christmas season is an opportune time to experience that abundance as we renew and recommit ourselves to our associations one with another. Christmas is a time for people more than presents.

On occasion I still catch myself feeling much like Phil Garland. Sometimes I may think that it is just another Christmas, that Christmas is too commercialized, and the price of toys and gifts is much, much too high.

But then I remember *Precious Jeopardy* and realize that there will be no other time exactly like this year for me and my family to celebrate this particular Christmas. Situations and people change with the seasons. And most importantly, I am just glad to be alive.

Our children are growing up, their grandparents are getting older, and we now realize that each Christmas is unique. We hope we will be able to spend many more Christmas seasons together, for it is, indeed, a time for rejoicing, renewal, and reflecting.

My needle is mounted on velvet and placed on our dresser as a constant reminder of the uncertainty of life and the importance of priorities. It is a precious gift, one I will always remember.

Brent A. Barlow, associate professor of family sciences at Brigham Young University, is the author of Twelve Traps in Today's Marriage—And How to Avoid Them, What Husbands Expect of Wives, *and* What Wives Expect of Husbands. *This article was previously published as "A Tiny Fragment of Steel" in the* Ensign, *December 1981.*

THE MEANING OF CHRISTMAS

by Lowell L. Bennion

The meaning of Christmas to me—like many important aspects of living—changes over time.

As a child, I was interested in what I might receive for Christmas. My brother and I searched the closets to find what our parents had stashed away until Christmas. One year we found a football and played with it before Christmas, carefully putting it back where we found it—unknown to our parents. Thanks to older brothers, I can't remember ever believing in Santa Claus.

The next meaning of Christmas to me was the spirit of giving. I was a missionary in Germany, serving as a senior companion in a small branch in Minden. We were invited to return to Bielefeld for Christmas Eve, the place of my previous assignment and labor. It was a tempting offer because there were many Saints there, good food, young people, and music.

But my companion and I decided to ride our bikes on Christmas Eve to Buckeburg, some thirty kilometers from Minden. There we would honor Christmas by spending the evening with two

sisters, one in bed with arthritis, the other, her nurse who stayed on with her, living in virtual poverty, because she was needed. The nurse had gone to work for the other lady when the latter was well-to-do, but inflation had reduced her to a very small income.

We sent these sisters a letter announcing our coming to give them the full pleasure of our visit.

Upon arrival, we knocked on the back door. The nurse opened it and invited us in through the kitchen. To our surprise, the kitchen table was set with a beautiful cloth and china from prosperous days long gone. We were served an elegant Christmas dinner, a goose with all the trimmings. When we left to go home, we were given a package with goodies, soap, and lotion.

Needless to say, I didn't enjoy the evening. I wondered where the nurse obtained money for our dinner and presents. I learned later that she had a sister who worked as a maid in Federal Heights in Salt Lake City. This sister had sent our hostess money to buy herself some shoes. Instead, she had spent her gift on us. That was the last time I dared to feel generous and pleased with my giving.

While giving in a selfless, spontaneous attitude of mind is a good way to express the Christmas spirit, a better way to celebrate Christmas is to honor Him whose birthday it is, to contemplate and be grateful for the wonderful life of Jesus and for all that He means to us. Let me recall some of the things that excite me about the life of Jesus of Nazareth.

Jesus was person-minded. His greatest loyalty was to His Father in heaven and to His fellow human beings. He went about doing good—healing the sick, making the blind to see and the deaf to hear and the lame to walk. He cleansed the lepers and liberated the minds of those thought to be possessed. He even raised the dead to comfort the bereaved.

So great was His interest in and love for people that there "drew near unto him all the publicans and sinners for to hear him." (Luke 15:1.) He gave sinners assurance of forgiveness and promised the poor a place in the kingdom of God. Jesus could also be firm and critical of the self-righteous and of those who neglected the great fundamentals of religion. "Woe unto you, scribes and Pharisees, hypocrites! for ye pay tithe of mint and anise and cummin, and have omitted the weightier matters of the law, judgment, mercy, and faith: these ought ye to have done, and not to leave the other undone." (Matthew 23:23.)

Jesus came not to destroy the law but to fulfill it. Anyone who would live the two great commandments—to love God and love neighbor—would automatically keep the Ten Commandments but also do more in many positive ways.

For Jesus, the law of Moses was not an end in itself to be obeyed and respected in the abstract. The law was given to bless people's lives. Even as a physician draws upon particular drugs and procedures to heal specific illnesses, so Jesus drew upon certain principles to heal the spiritual illnesses of people. This is illustrated beautifully in His relationship to the commandment to honor the sabbath. When criticized for healing (i.e., working) on the sabbath, Jesus said: "I will ask you one thing; Is it lawful on the sabbath days to do good, or to do evil? to save life, or to destroy it?" (Luke 6:9.)

On another occasion, his critics sought to trap him by bringing a woman caught in adultery and saying to him: "Master, this woman was taken in adultery, in the very act. Now Moses in the law commanded us, that such should be stoned: but what sayest thou?" Jesus replied, "He that is without sin among you, let him first cast a stone at her."

After his critics had walked away, "being convicted by their own conscience," Jesus said unto her: "Woman, where are those thine accusers? hath no man condemned thee? She said, No man, Lord. And Jesus said unto her, Neither do I condemn thee: go, and sin no more." (See John 8:3-11.)

Jesus' concept of the sinfulness of

adultery was even stricter than that of His critics, but the woman in this incident needed encouragement rather than condemnation. Jesus, sensitive to her needs, gave her comfort and hope.

It is so easy to think of religion in terms of beliefs, doctrines, and the Church, that we sometimes forget that the gospel was designed to bless the lives of people. It is refreshing to observe how Jesus related the gospel to meeting the needs of individuals.

For me, Jesus is the Master Teacher of religious and moral values. Many qualities made Him a great teacher. I will mention only a few.

Jesus taught fundamental principles such as love of God and love of neighbor (see, for example, Matthew 22). He said that everything depended on these two things. His eight Beatitudes build on each other in basic ways. The first four are elements of integrity; the last four, expressions of love. Because He taught profound principles such as faith, humility, integrity, and love, they have universal application that has lasted through time.

Jesus was an unequaled artist in His manner of teaching. No one has equaled Him in the creation of parables and proverbs. He wrote of things we can touch and see—of lilies in the field, of a sower who cast his seed on stony places among thorns or by the wayside where fowls devoured them.

Jesus exemplified His teaching by living a life of faith and trust, humility, meekness, moral courage, and by loving even His enemies.

I know for myself from observation and from testing His principles, sometimes succeeding in a measure and more often falling short, that they are true, good, and life-fulfilling.

I will celebrate the birth of Christ because He is my redeemer from sin and death. He reveals to me my sins by teaching me what is right. He "bringeth about means unto men that they may have faith unto repentance." (Alma 34:15.) So great is His love for His people that He suffers anguish over their wickedness. I will try to follow Him more truly to ease His suffering.

The most remarkable and miraculous thing I can imagine is the literal resurrection of the body. Jesus died that all might, like Him, rise again. While this promise staggers my imagination and tests my faith, I believe in its reality. His religious teachings are so true that I trust what He says about the promise of eternal life as well.

This Christmas I will think of Jesus and what He has given to me and to all human beings. I will celebrate His birth with hope, joy, and gratitude, for He is my Teacher, my Exemplar, and my Redeemer. Praise to His holy name!

Lowell L. Bennion, director of the Salt Lake Community Services Council, has made important contributions to LDS literature. His books include The Book of Mormon: A Guide to Christian Living; I Believe; Understanding the Scriptures; Jesus, the Master Teacher; The Unknown Testament; *and* The Things That Matter Most.

A PICTURE-PERFECT CHRISTMAS

by Janene Wolsey Baadsgaard

Every year about this time, I eagerly thumb through the women's magazines for ideas on how to have a happy Christmas. The slick, ink-scented, full-color pages are always brimming with such wonderful ideas.

You can almost smell golden glazed turkeys and butter-rich pastries heaped on elegant dining room tables. My own young family's limited Christmas dinner budget can usually afford an extra hot dog per child.

The little girls in the magazines are always dressed in deep plum velvets or silky white taffeta or in layers of eyelet lace and satin ribbons. The little boys are dressed in knee-length dark blue knickers with cotton white knee socks and shiny black patent leather shoes. I usually have a hard time keeping my children's raggedy undershirts tucked in their patched pants that they always grow out of too soon.

The Christmas trees in the magazines are always decorated with dazzling lights, bright poinsettias, or delicate, light-catching glass and porcelain ornaments. Our family Christmas tree is usually decorated with egg-carton, tin-foil bells.

"But this year," I always promise myself, "we'll have one of those picture-perfect Christmases."

Things never seem to work out the way I plan. Every year, it seems, there is another new stocking to hang up on the mantle, and the money has all gone to our obstetrician and pediatrician. We keep our local diaper manufacturer in business. Our little "stocking stuffers" are usually very soft, very pink newborns.

But each year after thumbing through those magazine pages of sparkle and lace, I wonder if maybe I'm missing something.

Before we tuck the children into bed on Christmas Eve, we pull out the family Bible and read the simple tale in our own words to our young, small, wide-eyed children. Each year the children eagerly ask to act out the story.

Every year or two, the children have a new brother or sister to take the part of "baby Jesus" in this annual ad-lib family Christmas program. The five-year-old carefully instructs the two-year-old on how to wear the bathroom towel so he can be Joseph, while the four-year-old runs to her room to find her stuffed lamb for the stable.

Our newest addition to the family is then gently wrapped in a worn flannel blanket while "Mary," our five-year-old, sings a lullaby she learned at Sunday School. The four-year-old can't decide if she wants to be the shepherd, angel, or wise man, so she usually runs from one part to the other, trying to do all three.

The five-year-old turns out the house lights after my husband lights a candle. The soft candle glow sparkles in our two-year-old Joseph's eyes as he holds the dusty kitchen broom in his sticky fingers for a staff. The worn gold carpet in the living room makes a nice manger of hay.

My children are dressed in mismatched pajamas instead of taffeta and velvet. But as I watch them there, the picture-perfect magazine Christmas seems only a tinsel illusion compared to my rich reality.

Janene Wolsey Baadsgaard, a columnist for Salt Lake City's Deseret News, *has published articles in the* Ensign *and* New Era *magazines. She is the author of* A Sense of Wonder, Is There Life After Birth? *and* Why Does My Mother's Day Potted Plant Always Die?

MOM WAS REALLY SANTA CLAUS

by Dennis L. Lythgoe

My mother's personality had a playful streak that caused her to seem childlike at times—even like one of us. As I look back, this seems consistent with her unparalleled excitement at Christmastime. We could always feel the intensity building toward the end of November and reaching a crescendo the night we picked out our Christmas tree. When it came to picking out a tree, Mom and I were kindred spirits. We preferred it bushy, not too tall or too short, and with no bad branches at all. This meant that we needed the entire evening, stopping at numerous tree merchants before we could find just the right tree—the ideal. The process drove my father crazy, but he waited and waited until we had found the perfect "bush" to bring home.

With the tree in the house and the aroma filling the living room, the Christmas spirit became infectious. Mom's optimism permeated the home. She did a lot of shopping, afterwards stashing strangely camouflaged parcels and bags in closets and under beds in our modest Salt Lake City home. She decorated the house and told Christmas stories, personal ones about her girlhood. Her own childhood had been spartan, and all her Christmas stories proved that she had been essentially deprived.

That was undoubtedly a major reason Christmas was so important to her in her adult years. Although my father worked for the railroad and never made very much money, Mom figured out an impressive way to play Santa Claus. (After she died at the age of seventy-seven, my sister and I found numerous caches of money deposited in little boxes and drawers in various dark corners of the house. Dad was as surprised as we were. It was obvious that we had discovered her "Christmas secret.")

We always opened one gift on Christmas Eve, a little exercise that made it slightly easier to sleep through the night. Mom's excitement seemed almost greater than ours. In bed, I would toss and turn and listen to strange noises emanating from the living room, wondering why Mom and Dad seemed to go to bed so late on Christmas Eve. Then I would drift a little, and suddenly it would be five o'clock in the morning, and I would leap out of bed and round up my brother and sisters. We would go into Mom and Dad's bedroom and Mom would enthusiastically rise while Dad would unsuccessfully implore us to sleep a little longer. If not, would we mind if he stayed in a few more minutes? "Of course not," we would say, "but not too long or you will miss it!" Invariably, he *did* roll over long enough to miss much of it.

But Mom was perched on the end of the overstuffed chair next to the Christmas tree, anxiously awaiting our reactions to the gifts. There would be several unwrapped items that were obvious, with names attached. A new dress hanging on a hanger on a lamp that said "Mary"; a sportcoat and slacks marked "Tom"; an adorable doll that said "Gaye"; and a bicycle parked in the middle of the floor labeled "Dennis." These were the big-ticket items she hoped would make us the happiest. If we did not say very much, she would gently probe, seeking reassurance that the gift was what we had in mind, or teaching us that Santa had trouble sometimes finding a certain gift.

For me the year of the bicycle was the most exciting. I had learned to ride a bike by borrowing one belonging to Vilate Nelson across the street. Because it was a girl's bike, it was easier for me to experiment on when I wasn't sure that I could stay up. I was intoxicated by the feeling, so every day I would go across the street to borrow the bike again. But it became steadily more em-

barrassing for me to ask, so when Christmas morning came and a full-size red bicycle stood on its kickstand next to the Christmas tree, I was exhilarated—and unbelievably grateful to Santa Claus for realizing the depth of my desire. The expansive smile on Mom's face that morning should have given me a deeper message, but I was too naive to catch on.

Clearly, Mom never expected any credit for her secret good deeds, and she cared little about her own gifts. We had to prod her into opening them while she was lost in her children's joy. All of us were amazed at the excitement Mom generated every Christmas season, and we sometimes tried to understand why our friends' mothers never seemed to compare. They always seemed so *old*.

Then one day one of those well-meaning classmates confided to me what she announced as a great truth which she had known for at least a year. "You should understand," she said with authority, "that Santa Claus is really just your parents." I had never considered such a radical possibility, and I hotly denied it. But by the end of the day I badly needed reassurance from someone who could speak with more authority—namely, Mother. I hurried in from school and found Mom putting some final decorating touches on the tree with my older brother.

"It isn't true, is it?" I asked desperately, quickly recounting my friend's frightening argument. Silence. For what seemed like a very long time, Mom said nothing. What's more, my brother Tom, who looked at me intently, did not seem shocked. Finally, Mom gently explained to me the traditional things that parents do for their children because they love them and because they want to feed the Christmas spirit. "Giving to someone you love when you know you won't be found out is the real joy of Christmas," she said. "And it's more exciting to give than to receive. You'll find that out someday."

Immediately, I understood. It must have been difficult for her to see my childlike belief fade, but she knew that if I ever asked the question she would have to be honest. Yet Christmas at our house became even richer in spiritual and family meaning, because I understood my mother's inner voice. I think that all of us emulate our parents' behavior with our own children, whether for good or ill, and my mother's Christmas traditions and spirit have lived not only in my home, but in the homes of my brother and sisters. We were all profoundly affected by her approach, and whenever that electric feeling of excitement that is identified with the Christmas season is expressed, I think of Mom.

Dennis Lythgoe, chairman of the Department of History at Bridgewater State College near Boston, is the author of The Sensitive Leader, A Marriage of Equals, *and* Let 'Em Holler: A Political Biography of J. Bracken Lee.

CHRISTMAS SNOWS, CHRISTMAS WINDS

by Don Marshall

The snow fell today in the streets where trucks and buses spun it into a gray wet spray and left it splattered on parked cars and curbs, pant legs and soggy shoes; and I feel that it must be falling now too somewhere on the fields and the fence posts, and that somewhere out there tonight when the light turns an icy blue and the dusty snow slithers along the highway like smoke, a black horse standing still in a white field will suddenly shiver and ripple its mane, and maybe a lone figure in coat and overshoes will trudge across that cold expanse with a pail of oats, puffs of steam trailing in the brittle air.

I passed a window where the head of an electric Santa Claus rotated from side to side. Along the crowded sidewalks a loudspeaker blared Fa-la-la-la-la over the muffled heads of passersby. In a crowd on a corner I saw a child licking at a clear red unicorn on a thin stick, and the snowflakes stung my cheeks and burned my eyes.

I remember those glass-candy animals; and I remember other things. I remember the days, the weeks, the months of waiting, interminable hours when December seemed worlds away. I remember tinseled moments even before October's leaves had turned to blue-gray smoke in the November air, when a sudden woody smell of pine or the far-off jingling of a bell sent crystal-shatters of Christmas tingling through my veins. I remember the smell of the new Sears and Roebuck catalogue when it came, and how the pages felt, and how, reaching with some inexplicable power through the endless blur of days ahead, it could steal a handful of Christmas and scatter it instantly, sugared and glittering, before us on the parlor rug where we lay. Every page was Christmas: even a simple plaid bathrobe became magically invested with holly berries and mistletoe, and an ordinary pair of socks triggered immediately a chorus of carolers accompanied by chimes.

I remember the long afternoons at school when the radiator hissed, and bare branches, black against a chalky sky, made soft tapping noises at the windows. Weary of making crayon Christmases on sheets of paper, I would let my pencil plow a little furrow of dirt from the cracks in the floor while I longed for the passing of weeks and waited for that special day. And we would practice the songs for the Christmas program, and I would squirm restlessly on the little painted chairs, excited by the visions conjured by musical fragments—the little town of Bethlehem lying so still with its dreamless sleep and its silent stars, the three kings bearing gifts and traveling from afar, and, perhaps the most glorious of all in those days, jolly old Saint Nicholas leaning his ear and promising not to tell a single soul.

After the endless days of painting and cutting and pasting and shellacking, the secret gifts—plaster of paris plaques or wind chimes of glass rectangles dangling by yarn from a Kerr lid—would lie drying on the low shelves by the radiator, while we filed, in homemade costumes of rabbits or snowflakes, tin soldiers or shepherds, into the little rows of chairs to perform at last before the nebulous faces of relatives and townspeople in the darkened auditorium. "Hark, the herald angels sing!" we chanted, the words to most of the carols garbled even to us, and our minds forever straying to the glossy images in the Sears catalogue. Then the program would be over and there would be no more going back to school for almost two weeks, yet the waiting would go on, only now it would continue in the home—watching from the parlor windows for the first sign of a snowflake, carefully printing the letter

and trusting it would reach the North Pole in time, studying the blacked flue of the fireplace and wondering how the whole miraculous thing could possibly be brought about.

I remember the days of Christmas-card-making, my materials strewn out on the rug or set up temporarily on a bridge table but inevitably before the fireplace so that I could savor the piney smell and be as near as possible to the popping and crackling fire, its sizzling sap seeming to whisper, "It's coming, it's coming, it's coming!" I recall the snips and scraps of colored paper; the homemade cards with cut-out windows; the obligatory winter scenes drawn laboriously with colored pencils, the village houses and steepled churches somehow owing more to calendar Vermonts than to the Marysvales and Junctions and Circlevilles strung around me.

I remember helping to shake the snow from the tree propped frozen against the porch and running behind as Papa and my brothers dragged it inside through the door, fearing that its branches would be broken and lamenting that its trunk must be shortened. I remember my uneasiness as they grafted boughs in the empty spaces and my surprise and my joy at discovering pine cones and maybe even a bird's nest hidden somewhere in its upper branches. I loved the dusty-sweet and spicy smell loaned by the tree to the parlor; I loved even the sugary pine gum that stuck to my fingers and resisted soap and water, giving way finally only to the salty slipperiness of

71

Mama's butter. And when the dusty boxes were brought up from the basement and opened on the parlor rug, I loved the smell of candles as we unwrapped them from their crumpled tissue; I loved seeing each tangle of colored lights finally glow against the rug as we tightened every globe and tried each string in the socket to discover which burnt-out bulb was holding back the others; and I loved rediscovering each ornamental bell and ball, old friends momentarily forgotten since that January day nearly a year before when they were wrapped between the Sunday pages of *Maggie and Jiggs* and *Little Orphan Annie* and tucked away in shoeboxes to await December's resurrection. In those days our decorations were a melange of Christmases past and all the dearer for the memories they evoked; almost no ornaments — from the magenta foil cone awaiting candy and nuts to the fragile glass bird with the spunglass tail — were alike, and the tree lights themselves, many enhanced by metallic reflectors in the shape of water lilies or stars, ranged from a rotund little Santa Claus to an intricate and marvelous Chinese lantern. And when each member of this bizarre menagerie had found a hospitable bough, and when all the foil icicles had been hung until they dripped, silver and shimmering, from almost every needle, we hid the homemade tree stand under a cotton matting, sprinkled it with glistening mica flakes, and set up on its snowy whiteness a miniature cardboard village, a colored bulb in each tiny house glowing softly through a doorway or stained-glass window.

I remember that spicy piney scent suddenly mingling with the smell of whole cloves and cinnamon bark simmering in the hot juices of apples, pineapples, lemons, and oranges that would become wassail to be ladled out in steaming cups for all visitors; and I remember it mingling with the smell of mincemeat pies and rhubarb pies as they bubbled in the oven, and with the smell of doughnuts sizzling in oil, waiting to be fished out and rolled in sugar and eaten hot. I remember peeking over the breadboard as the cranberries and oranges oozed through the grinder to become a sweet relish that tasted like Christmas; I remember the nuts and candied fruit dropping into the spicy batter that would be poured into pans and transformed into golden-brown fruitcakes inside the oven. I remember the annual appearance in the kitchen of figs and dates, an exotic touch of the East that suddenly seemed as right and as welcome as the camel-borne kings parading across our mantel amidst the pine boughs and scented candles.

By Christmas Eve the mound of presents growing under the tree had almost obscured the cardboard village, and each ribboned package there for more than one day had been rubbed and poked and pinched from every angle. But it was what was not there that we waited for most — not the hastily wrapped shapes that would inevitably appear at the last minute on that final eve, but those other things, finally

72

placed unwrapped and glittering in the glow of colored lights, that would never appear until we had eventually drifted off to sleep, with or without visions of sugarplums.

A snowfall on that eve of eves had seemed beyond question, and I remember standing one year in my pajamas looking with incredulity through the window at only a gray-blue bleakness settling in on the dead and naked grass. Santa Claus's sleigh, even flying through the stars, seemed unnecessary and impossible without that obligatory frosty whiteness that had to fall and cover the world. And fall it did. As I pressed a wet cheek against the cold glass, feeling somehow cheated, I saw the first tiny flakes, like lint fluttering in the wind, slithering down the cold blue sky. How necessary it was! In order for the miracle of Christmas to be, the everydayness of mud ruts and frozen gutters *had* to be lost under the sparkling magic of snow.

I remember the snow and I remember other things. I remember the year my stocking hung alone on the string by the fire. My brothers and sisters, suddenly grown away from such things, had turned to dances and caroling atop a horse-drawn hay wagon, and I would peek out of the window into the frosty night, at the faintest rustling of bells, to see them pass or hear them singing above the steady clopping of the mare's hooves on the icy road. From my window, too, I could see down the block to the giant Christmas tree erected in the middle of town. I

could see its lights reflected in the shiny whiteness of the street, and I could watch late shoppers balancing packages as they crept carefully across the ice, calling last-minute wishes to passing friends and then disappearing into the cold night.

I remember lying in my bed under the heavy blankets, wanting to capture every sound—Would I hear a tap-tap on the roof or a slithering down the chimney or the clicking of a cup on a saucer as Santa drank the milk and ate the doughnut left for him by the fire?—yet I longed at the same time for sleep to come quickly in order to make the night disappear and the morning come. And when I awoke in the stillness of that blue-violet hour separating night and morning and crept down the darkened hall and through the front room, I always stood entranced on the threshold of the parlor. What other moment could match that moment as I hesitated, scarcely breathing, my eyes taking in the pure magic of each carefully placed and glistening item reflecting the still-burning tree lights and the rosy warmth of the still-smoldering fire, and retaining yet some vestige of the aura surrounding the white-bearded figure whose hand had placed them there—and left only a few sugary crumbs on the saucer by the hearth—perhaps only minutes before?

Careful not to break the spell, I would kneel down quietly to examine, first with my eyes and then with my fingers, each precious piece of a farm set with its hard-rubber pigs and cows, or—another year—a rustic fort with metal Indians and cavalry; once the featured item was a set of Tinker Toys, another time Lincoln Logs, and, still another, a shiny and complicated Erector Set. This was the special hour, that quiet hour before dawn, the room bewitched by the lights of the tree and the only sound an occasional popping of a spark or the soft shifting of coals as the pine logs, now charcoal, crumbled into rose-gold embers. I worshipped this hour, these enchanted moments, when Christmas and I touched, and nothing broke the spell. Even the taking down of my stocking, which now bulged lumpily and heavily on the sagging string, was a ritual. As I turned it upside down, emptying the contents into the lid of a box, I loved every nut, every piece of ribbon candy or multicolored hardtack, even the silver quarter that sometimes rolled down among the cream-centered chocolate Bunker Hills and the inevitable glass-candy Santa Claus or lion or unicorn. There would be an orange, too, and though it was exactly like those colder ones from the kitchen, it seemed marvelous and special; for just as the little nut-covered balls with the cream centers or the pastel-colored sugary mounds were identical to those in bowls on the bookcase, just as each almond and pecan and brazil nut, still in its shell, was no different from those waiting in the wooden bowl with the nutcracker, each one, like the orange, had been blessed by the hands of Santa Claus, and each one had been placed

there especially for me.

Later on in the morning, when the parlor rug was lost under a storm of wrapping paper and ribbon, we would take turns winding the phonograph to hear Bing Crosby sing "White Christmas" and "Happy Holiday," and the smell of roasting pheasant or duck—shot the day before by one of my brothers—would be drifting from the kitchen while neighbors and uncles and aunts were stomping the snow from their feet outside the door and bursting in, arms full of presents, shouting out the greetings that we all loved. I never tired of showing one more time that marvelous portion of the chaos under the tree that was mine alone, and only in the late afternoon, when I lay drowsily on the rug before the fire and the house was quiet again, would I feel the melancholy seeping in, the sad thought that night was coming on and then it would be tomorrow and tomorrow would be Christmas no more.

But there is something else I remember, too. Sometimes I forgot it—always I try to forget it—but it keeps coming back like a cold and brittle wind. It claims a part of those Christmas memories, too—a part not willed to it or even acknowledged. Unwelcome guest in that memory world of gumdrops and candy canes, it sneaks along the edges of the mind, demanding it be seen, heard, remembered. It is always there, tapping at the back windows like branches in the night.

There was a German family that had a farm a few miles from our town. We scarcely knew them for they spoke little and their English was poor and broken. But we would see them in the town in their faded pickup—the old man with dried manure on his boots, the woman with frightened eyes and a yellowish braid wound around her head. They had a daughter a year or two younger than I, a very quiet girl with pale skin and pale hair, who wore hand-me-downs and moved through the halls of school with scarcely a word. Her English was probably as good as mine, yet we never somehow remembered it that way. We referred to her derisively as Consolation; her real name was Helga or Inger or something like that, but we always called her Consolation because someone, I think, had seen her once with her arm around a child who had hurt his knee on the playground. Sometimes she too wore braids around her head, and then she looked like a strange little mother, grown old before her time. She never had any close friends as I recall, yet we often linked her name, in jest, with anyone we wanted to tease or get back at for something they had done.

One Christmas, when my friends and I were struggling to announce our maturity to the world (no stockings by the fire that year), we slid on the ice and wrestled in the snow outside the schoolhouse until the last cars had driven up in the dark, and the program had already begun with a rousing carol. We then trudged in, during that opening number, and noisily appropriated some empty seats on the front row. We poked each other while the second graders bellowed "Hark, the Herald Angels Sing" in bathrobe-and-towel shepherd costumes, and we traded whispered comments and stifled giggles at the fourth-grade angel with one wing flopping and at Mary with her tinseled halo askew. Then suddenly the junior high band was performing "O Holy Night," and Consolation, we realized to our great mirth, was playing a brief French horn solo. It began wobbly, two or three of the notes were blurbled, and once she even seemed to falter as though she had lost her place. We snickered, and tried, unsuccessfully, to pinch our legs to keep from laughing outright. She finally finished, her frightened eyes, resembling her mother's, dropping to her music stand and never leaving it until the program ended. When it was over and we pushed our way through the crowd outside to where car doors slammed and sputtering engines sent up clouds of white exhaust, we passed by the faded pickup, and I saw the old man there in the dark with his arm around the girl. She was sobbing against the heaviness of his mackinaw, and the woman was soothing her hand over the girl's braids. "Race ya to the corner!" somebody yelled, and we took off, slipping and sliding on the ice and into the night.

Today the snow fell in the streets, and cars slipped and slid and spun around, snarling traffic at every corner. The sidewalks are lost under a gray-brown slush, but maybe the snow will mercifully continue to fall and cover it all. Maybe down the highway where the snow blows like smoke across the road and a lone horse shivers in the wind, the snow will be thick and deep and white. Consolation, where are you now that the snow is falling once again on the fences and the fields? I didn't cry for you then, but I cry for you now.

Don Marshall is the author of the novel Zinnie Stokes, Zinnie Stokes *as well as two collections of short stories,* Frost in the Orchard *and* The Rummage Sale. *"Christmas Snows, Christmas Winds" was previously published in* Frost in the Orchard, *Deseret Book, 1985.*

THE CHRISTMAS LETTER

by Karla C. Erickson

One Christmas several years ago when our children were all young, a sudden realization dawned. Whenever a gift was placed under the tree, they scampered to see the name tag. The child whose name was on the package grabbed the gift and quickly put it into "his" pile. Each was ecstatic when he or she accumulated the most presents. It took no genius to realize the true meaning of Christmas was certainly missing. I explained that it feels better to give gifts than to receive them. Unbelieving grins crossed their faces as if to say, "Sure, Mom."

The following Christmas my husband and I decided to try another approach. After a shopping spree with the children, they wrapped their gifts for their brothers and sisters. But instead of distributing the presents, each kept the gifts he was giving in "his" pile.

Early Christmas morning, after our family prayer, we focused the camera on the children as they hurried down the stairs. After examining the gifts left by Santa, we gathered in a circle. The youngest child gathered her pile of gifts and proceeded to hand out each present. One at a time, in order of age, each family member opened the gift she'd given them. She stood watching the event to see if her gift would please the recipient. A hug, kiss, and "thanks" were cherished rewards.

The camera captured the event on film, but we all captured the feeling within. The next youngest child then gathered his gifts to give.

Our children experienced the joy of giving. The moments were unhurried. Not one child said, "Aren't there any more presents to open?"

Many years have passed since that Christmas morning, but our tradition continues. Last Christmas provided an enduring family memory. When it came to our third youngest, age nine, to give her gifts, she quickly rushed to her room and returned with a handful of letters. She gathered her pile of gifts, and as she gave each one a present she also gave them a letter. She explained, "I wanted to give you something special this year. Something I couldn't buy. So I wrote you each a Christmas letter." We each, one at a time, opened her gift and then read out loud her letter.

When it came to our eighteen-year-old son, the eldest, he read: "Dear Jeff, This is our last Christmas together for a long time. It's not going to be fun without you taking me places like: The Jazz game. The Symphony. And Restaurants. You are so nice to me. I love you very much. Love, Kelli. P.S. Next year I still will send you a present."

With a mission awaiting Jeff, Kelli reminded us that never again will we share the Christmas holidays as we have in the past. With missions, schooling, marriages, and even grandchildren someday, our family circle will be altered.

Those treasured letters reminded us of the laughter and fun we have shared around our Christmas tree. They reminded us of the love felt for one another. They were proof that love and giving is what Christmas is all about.

Someday when my husband and I are the only ones by the lighted tree on Christmas morning, maybe our grandchildren will be gathering their piles of gifts to give to their brothers and sisters and mother and father. And if they are fortunate, perhaps they will receive a Christmas letter.

Karla C. Erickson is the author of Gifts Only You Can Give, Take Time to Smell the Dandelions, Kids in the Kitchen, *and* Invest in the Best, Your Kids.

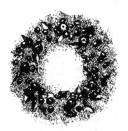

ANTICIPATION OF
THE SHEPHERDS

by Richard Tice

Awe-laden shepherds, did your watch by night
anticipate the sudden angel all ablaze?
Did your fluted lullabies delight
better than seraphic skies of praise?
Did abiding by your flocks with care
prepare you for the guardian of your souls?

Newly born shepherd, are you as yet aware
of quests for strays among ravines and knolls?
Of how reverberating anthems of acclaim
will lead you to a lonely psalm of grace?
Of how your throne encircled by angelic flame
gave way to dark, with only straw for an embrace?

Both young and old, in shepherd-like felicity,
as man to child and child to man, grow perfectly.

ALL THE PROPHETS

by Richard Tice

I am old—
so near is death against the birth
that was foretold.

I am dying
before the chilling grave that I await,
my trust relying.

I am patient,
for though I die I know the hope
the promise meant;

And I am waiting
in the crowded Court of Gentiles
for my rightful king.

I am here,
to hold within my arms this child
whom I revere.

I am Simeon,
who saw in flesh what prophets saw
in distant vision.

(Luke 2:22–35.)

THIS OLD BIBLE

by Richard Tice and Jack Lyon

this old Bible: the "I"
illuminates "In the beginning"

"The lesser light
to rule the night" —
moonlight on the pages

(first link by Richard Tice,
second link by Jack Lyon)

Richard Tice is an assistant editor for the Ensign *magazine and editor and publisher of* Dragonfly, *a magazine on haiku. He has also published a novel,* The Inside Track, *and a book of poetry,* Station Stop.
Jack Lyon is an associate editor at Deseret Book Company and an editor of Dragonfly.

CHRISTMAS AWAY FROM HOME

by Mary Ellen Edmunds

It was my fourth Christmas away from home. The first was in Taiwan, then there were two in the Philippines. I wondered what the season would be like in a country where the predominant religion was Islam. My companion and I arrived in Indonesia early in November 1976. Sister Low was a Chinese girl born in Malaysia who had lived in England for several years. We stayed in Jakarta, the capital, for a few weeks and had our first taste of the Christmas season.

We were invited to a private school to watch the arrival of "Sinterklaus." Everyone gathered in the playground area with much anticipation and many cameras. Soon two men called "Black Peter" arrived on a Harley-Davidson motorcycle, waving and throwing little biscuits to the crowd. Then a helicopter began circling overhead and everyone got more excited. The chopper landed, and inside was Sinterklaus himself, decked out in a magnificent costume. Everyone moved towards the big pavilion for a program. We didn't have time for that, so we turned to leave.

And then I saw them—the little Indonesian children without shoes, crowding as close as they dared or were allowed to come, eyes wide with the wonder of what they saw and heard. It struck me forcefully: the wide, wide separation between these two groups of children. Some of the parents of the school children looked at these other children in disgust with a "why-do-they-have-to-interrupt-our-private-celebration" kind of expression. There was sad irony in this scene—welcoming Sinterklaus and the Christmas season with songs and words about happiness, goodwill toward men, love and giving, but trying to prevent a gang of ragged little children from "getting too close." This was the beginning of the Christmas of 1976—for me one of the most unusual of my life.

That afternoon, December 3, we got on a train and headed for Solo, Central Java. I sat by the window and watched the people and wondered about their lives and their "holiday season." I saw people living in all sorts of shelters, even cardboard boxes that reminded me of the "forts" we used to build in the backyard in the summer. I watched people carrying water, feeding babies, carrying heavy loads on their backs.

The train wasn't quite like the Pullmans we used to ride to California to visit our cousins. I was the only Anglo on the entire train. It was great trying to walk between the cars on our way to and from our dinner of soup and rice—one wrong step and your leg was outside. It reminded me of something that would go over big at Disneyland. As I got in my upper berth at bedtime I kept wishing I could take a picture—I was flat on my back with my nose ten inches from the ceiling.

We arrived in Solo and began to get settled. In the first meeting we attended with the members of the Church I understood one word: *pohon* (tree). I was discouraged until I learned that the members had been speaking in Javanese, their native language, rather than Indonesian, which we had learned. But understanding the word *tree* gave me the idea they were going to get a Christmas tree, and they did. We went with the members of the branch to Tawan-manggu, in a mountainous region near Solo. We met many friendly people and took pictures of wild monkeys. The tree we got was huge, beautiful, and crooked.

We made an effort to make our little home look like Christmas. We hung up both of our Christmas cards as soon as we arrived and added others as they found us. Sister Low had a tape of Jim Reeves singing Christmas songs, and we played it over and over. On Christmas Eve a sound truck went up and

down the streets of Solo with a *loud* version of the Lennon Sisters singing, "I'm dreaming of a white Christmas." I listened to the words and thought about home, family, friends, traditions, and all that usually helped "make the season bright." Then I read the story of Christmas in English and in Indonesian, and reminded myself of the true significance of the season. I consciously thought of blessings instead of challenges. It was easy to think of the latter, because they surrounded us every day. Flea, bedbug, and mosquito bites. Scorpions and lizards and rats and cockroaches. No hot water. No sink. No toilet. I learned to chew softly because often there were rocks or other surprises in the rice.

I put a picture of Mom and Dad on my wall near my bed, and it became a source of peace and comfort—and encouragement—to look at them smiling at me and telling me everything would be all right, and "Merry Christmas." The more I thought about it, the more I realized that I had so *much* that millions and millions of people in Indonesia and the world didn't even know how to dream about. It changed my heart and my attitude.

On Christmas Eve we went to the little place we used for our chapel and celebrated with the members of the branch. Most had brought neighbors and friends, and there were probably close to *three hundred people* in our little building. The huge tree wound its way to the ceiling and was loaded with a unique variety of decorations. Cotton was spread out "here and there" for the snow effect. There were *two* "store-bought" decorations and eleven tiny bulbs that blinked briefly every twenty seconds.

The program was long and noisy and tremendous. There was a fifty-watt "spotlight" that hung from the ceiling and came on once in a while during the various productions. Someone had a doll to represent the Baby Jesus, and He lay in a manger made of leaves. As I looked around at everyone, with their Sunday-best clothes and their joy and excitement, I realized I was crying. The power failed during "Joy to the World," but we sang on with much emotion and filled with the real spirit of this wonderful season of Christmas. As we rode our bikes home on that peaceful, warm Christmas Eve, I was thinking of the words to the hymn, "Come Unto Jesus." The fourth verse shares this powerful, wonderful truth: "Come unto Jesus from ev'ry nation, From ev'ry land and isle of the sea. Unto the high and lowly in station, Ever he calls, 'Come to me, to me.' "

Mary Ellen Edmunds is associate director of training at the Missionary Training Center and is a member of the Relief Society General Board. This article was first published in This People *magazine, December 1986/ January 1987.*

CREATIVE HOLIDAY IDEAS

by Dian Thomas

Holiday Planning Calendar

Planning makes perfect during the holidays. At the beginning of the Christmas season, family members get together and list Christmas activities on a large appointment or desk-blotter-size calendar. Shopping trips with smaller children, parties, Christmas concerts, the day for tree selection and trimming—even Christmas-wrapping and cookie-baking sessions—are written on the calendar. Having holiday season activities available at a glance helps coordinate family plans.

Family Portrait Ornaments

Add a special ornament to the family Christmas tree each year. Have a family Christmas photograph taken annually. Make it into a Christmas tree ornament. This creates a wonderful tradition as well as a family photo history. Each ornament will be a valuable treasure as years pass and the family grows.

Hanging Gingerbread Men

String together gingerbread men as a tasty farewell treat for visitors. To make the string, roll out about twelve feet of plastic wrap. Place the decorated gingerbread men face down lengthwise about two inches apart along the wrap. Fold the wrap in from both sides, overlapping it to cover the gingerbread men. Use colorful red and green Christmas ribbons to tie a secure bow around the wrap between each gingerbread man. Top the string with a large, full bow. Hang your colorful string of gingerbread men next to the front door. As holiday guests leave, snip off a gingerbread treat for them to munch on their way.

Christmas Card Holder

Make your Christmas cards easy to read with this handy holder. Cut both ends from a tall, narrow can. Potato chip cans work well. Secure red or green yarn to the inside of the can with masking or filament tape. Wind the yarn up and down inside and outside of the can until the yarn completely covers it. Strips of yarn should be close together. Secure the end of the yarn to the inside of the can with another piece

of tape.

Slip the Christmas card under one strip of yarn so that the yarn holds it to the can along the fold of the card. The card hangs open and makes it easy to read special messages all through the holidays.

Wish Book

A special notebook will help everyone select gifts for other family members through the year. Prepare a notebook with a section for each person in the family. Each person's section includes a page for clothing sizes. Other pages list items needed and items wanted.

The notebook can be covered with fabric, wrapping paper, or contact paper. When ideas for presents are needed, family members can glance at the book and select a perfect gift. Keep the notebook and use it year after year. Save the "wish lists" to share and enjoy as years pass.

Christmas Tree in a Playpen

A Christmas tree is very attractive — especially to little ones. Try this idea, it could save your tree.

Put your decorated tree in a baby's playpen. Tree and packages will be safe and the little ones can still enjoy it. For a decorative touch, add a big bow to each corner of the playpen.

Making a Snowman

A jolly but delectable snowman can be made in any size.

1/2 cup butter or margarine
1 16-ounce package miniature marshmallows
1 teaspoon salt
20 cups popped popcorn
Black top hat
Candy for face and buttons

Melt butter or margarine in large saucepan over low heat. Add marshmallows and salt. Stir until completely melted. Continue stirring 3 minutes. Remove from heat. Pour over popped corn and stir until coated.

While mixture is still warm, shape with buttered fingers into large ball, medium ball, and small ball. To secure balls on top of one another, form small "bowl" in top of bottom ball and bump on bottom of middle ball. Do the same for two top balls. When balls are put together, bump fills bowl and holds balls in place.

Decorate with top hat, candy face, and candy buttons.

Dian Thomas launched her career with the best-selling Roughing It Easy. *Recognized nationally as an expert on creative living, and a regular on NBC's "Today Show," she has also written* More Roughing It Easy *and* Tips for Creative Living.

I KNOW WHO SANTA CLAUS IS

by Carroll Hofeling Morris

I was five when I found out there wasn't a real person named Santa Claus who lived at the North Pole with a fat wife, a herd of reindeer, and a work force of elves. No, I didn't catch the fattest person in our church struggling into a red suit the night of the Christmas party; I didn't see my mom kissing a somehow familiar Santa Claus under the mistletoe; my older brothers and sisters didn't ruin my childhood by telling me. I found out about Santa in an unusual fashion, and who knows how old I might have been before my disillusionment but for the fact that I was a confirmed thumb-sucker.

My sister said I sucked it because I was the baby of the family. My older brother's logic attributed it to the fact that I was born in Arizona (the others were born in Minneapolis). I myself didn't spend any time analyzing it. For me, it was simple—I loved my thumb. It was sweet, juicy, comforting. And in spite of the fact that it was often red and sore, sucking it was pure pleasure, necessary for going to sleep and for living through the trials common to five-year-old girls.

My parents didn't see it that way. They tried everything to get me to stop, with no success. Threats were useless, because I knew they were too soft-hearted to carry through with them. Their one attempt to do so had ended in a disaster they couldn't forget. They had painted my thumb with a hideous concoction supposed to make it taste too terrible to suck. They didn't notice how sore the end of my thumb was as they daubed the stuff on. The minute it touched the raw, pink skin I started screeching. I howled for hours until the combination of diligent washing and children's aspirin took the edge off the pain. So much for threats.

Bribes didn't work either. I think my parents kept offering them mostly because they felt somewhat better about bribes than threats. They promised me a trip to the amusement park, a cradle for my doll, and even a new bicycle if I would stop sucking my thumb. But I couldn't.

In desperation, Mom finally took the advice of her fellow high school German teacher, who suggested that she read me the poem about thumb-sucking in *Der Struwwelpeter. Der Struwwelpeter* was a book of poems they used in their classes describing the terrible consequences of bad behavior. Because nothing else she had tried had worked, Mom brought the book home from school with her.

The poem, which Mom translated as she went along, told the story of a little boy whose mother was going out. Her last-minute instruction to him was that he must not suck his thumb. But the moment she left, he popped his thumb into his mouth. Suddenly, a tailor appeared, brandishing a huge pair of shears. Snip, snap, he cut off both the boy's thumbs. At this point in the story, the illustrations showing the shears, the dripping blood, and the thumbless hands made Mother's translations unnecessary. I understood perfectly: Such are the wages of thumb-sucking.

In those days not much was being said about protecting little psyches, so my parents were unprepared for the effect their most recent cure had on me. I ran screaming to my room, clutching my thumb to me in terror. It took me a long time to go to sleep that night, and when I did, I dreamed of mutilation and woke up in hysterics. For the next week, I refused to go to bed unless my mother was by my side, protecting me from mad tailors wielding bloody shears.

I lived in fear for quite a while after that, sucking my thumb only when my face was hidden behind a book or under a blanket or pillow. But when noth-

ing unusual happened, my fear of the tailor gradually subsided, and things went back to normal. Until Uncle Fritz came to visit.

He was really Mom's uncle and my great-uncle. He was a bachelor who lived with my grandparents on a farm near New Ulm, Minnesota. I had never met him, but my brothers and sisters had told me a lot about him. They neglected to tell me one important thing, however, to their regret.

The day Uncle Fritz was to arrive we were all excited. "He's here!" Mom cried as the car drove up. Everybody ran out the front door, and I followed. Uncle Fritz (who was a tall man with a sunburned face, crinkly eyes, and a wide smile) was barely out of the car when Mom and my brothers and sister descended on him. A lot of laughing and hugging went on while Dad and I watched. When the rest of the family finally stepped back from Uncle Fritz a little, he shook hands with Dad. That done, he looked right at me with the nicest brown eyes I had ever seen. Mom pushed me toward him. "This is our Annie," she said.

I suppose he could tell I was shy, so he decided to shake my hand instead of hugging me. But instead of taking the hand he offered, I froze, my eyes wide with terror. There where his thumb should have been was a stump!

"Oh, dear," said Mom. "I forgot to tell her about your thumb."

Uncle Fritz grinned as he looked ruefully at his hand. "Poor old thumb," he said, shaking his head. "I lost it because I sucked it too much."

He was just trying to be funny, but the minute he said the words, a vision of him being cornered by the sadist with the shears flashed through my mind, and I started to bawl. Although both he and Mother tried to tell me he had really lost his thumb in a farm accident, I wasn't convinced. Needless to say, I didn't get to know Uncle Fritz very well on that visit.

My parents then tried a different tactic in regard to my habit. To this day I'm not sure if they read a new book on child behavior or just got tired. Whatever the reason, they gave me permission to suck my thumb all I wanted to.

Oddly enough, once permission had been granted, I sucked my thumb less. I cut back even more after I entered kindergarten in the fall, for fear of embarrassing myself in front of my classmates. Not long after that, I even began going to sleep without it. I had conquered my habit! With that realization, my fear of Uncle Fritz and the tailor faded—which was lucky, because Mom and Dad decided to take us to visit our grandparents and Uncle Fritz that Christmas.

"I get to see snow!" I exulted when they told me. I could hardly wait until we packed our car and set out for "Minnesota, land of 10,000 *frozen* lakes," as my father put it.

Even though I was in a frenzy of anticipation, I was unprepared for a landscape that looked like a laundry room disaster with mounds of spilled-over Tide covering everything. Nor was I

prepared for the cold. But that didn't deter us kids. We made snow angels, went sledding on the hill behind the barn, and skated on the stock pond. We stayed outside until our cheeks were raw and red.

And guess who was with us most of the time? Uncle Fritz. Now that I didn't suck my thumb anymore, his stump didn't bother me. And Uncle Fritz was fun to be around. He wasn't like other adults. When none of the others wanted to leave the snug kitchen for a snowball fight, he would. When everybody else was tired of "Chutes and Ladders," he was good for one more game. I began to understand why my brothers and sister liked him so much.

All the fun I was having didn't stop me from keeping track of the days until Christmas, however. When the day of the church Christmas program arrived, I knew the waiting was almost over. That night I would get to tell Santa Claus what I wanted for Christmas, and the next night, which was Christmas Eve, he would leave the requested gift under the tree in Grandma and Grandpa's living room.

Finally the moment came. Out from behind the royal blue stage curtains stepped a wonderful Santa, round and red and furry. He held up a red net Christmas stocking and announced that he had come to give just such a stocking to every girl and boy there.

I lost my sister in the general mayhem as all the kids rushed to line up, but I didn't care. I watched eagerly as the first stockings were handed out, measuring their size and trying to guess what was in them. Popcorn balls and nuts and candy, I decided.

The line moved with excruciating slowness, but finally I reached the stage steps and climbed them to the stage itself. Then it was my turn. I stepped right up to Santa and gave him my biggest smile.

"Hello, little girl," he said in a voice muffled by his beard. "What's your name?"

"Annie," I replied.

"Well, Annie, how do you like spending your Christmas where there's snow instead of cactus?"

I gasped. "How did you know there's cactus where I live?"

"Santa knows everything!" he said, smiling. He winked at me in a conspiratorial fashion and held out the stocking I had been waiting for—in a hand that was minus its thumb! My eyes jumped to the whiskered face, and I recognized the brownish eyes with laugh wrinkles around them. For a moment I was too shocked to move or speak. Then the boy next in line shoved me impatiently. I grabbed the stocking and without a word or smile ran back to my parents.

"I know who that Santa Claus is!" I said indignantly as I flopped down into my seat. "That Santa Claus isn't real. He's just Uncle Fritz."

They tried telling me that Uncle Fritz was an official substitute for the real Santa, who was stuck in a snowdrift outside Worthington, but it didn't do any good. I knew with sudden and absolute certainty that there was no such person as Santa Claus.

The word *conspiracy* was not a part of my vocabulary then, but I felt as if every adult in my life had conspired to convince me there was a Santa Claus. I had believed. I had given Santa all the love my five-year-old heart could hold. And I had been betrayed.

"Take your dumb old stocking," I said rudely, shoving it into my mother's hand. "I don't want a dumb old stocking from a fake Santa." I sat with crossed arms and primly pursed lips the rest of the evening and all the way home. But when I went to bed that night, I put my head under my pillow so my sister wouldn't hear me, and I cried.

The next morning I didn't get up when the rest of the family did. I could hear them talking and laughing in the kitchen, and delicious breakfast smells were making my nose twitch, but I couldn't bear the thought of being down there. How could they be so happy, knowing that there was no Santa? They must not have loved him as much as I had or they wouldn't have been able to accept his demise so casually. I, on the other hand, would never be happy again.

The bedroom door opened and my dad stuck his head inside the room. "Hey, lazy bones, bail out! Tonight's Christmas Eve!"

"I'm not getting up."

He quickly came over to the bed and pulled the covers down so he could see my face. "You're not sick, are you?"

I shook my head.

"Still sleepy?"

Again I shook my head.

"What is it then?" He smiled as he spoke, and that smile made me want to tell him, but I couldn't. I was afraid he would laugh at me. So I turned my back to him, and after a bit, I heard him leave the room.

Mom came in next. "What's the matter, dear?" she asked as she sat on the side of the bed.

"I don't want to get up," I blurted out. "I don't want it to be Christmas Eve."

"It's because of Santa, isn't it?"

I nodded, sniffling into my pillow. "I don't want to ever get up again if there isn't a Santa Claus."

"Oh, but there is a Santa Claus," my mother said. "There must be a thousand books about him, and why would people write so many books about someone who wasn't real?"

"To fool little children. I bet there isn't one grown-up who believes in Santa Claus."

"I do. He's real in my heart. He may not be a person like you and me, but he's real. He stands for the feeling I have when Christmas comes. He is the happiness I feel when I give to someone else."

That was too much for me. I snorted and burrowed back under the covers, refusing to listen to her. After a while my mother left, too.

It was like a parade after that. One after another, my brothers and sister and grandma and grandpa tried to coax me out of bed or to convince me that Christmas would still be the same even if I couldn't believe in Santa Claus anymore. When none of their arguments worked, they sent up Uncle Fritz.

"You're pretty mad, aren't you?" he said, his brown eyes crinkled into a smile.

I didn't answer.

"Well, I don't blame you."

"Why did you pretend to be Santa Claus last night?" I asked accusingly.

He shrugged. "Somebody had to. You see, Santa isn't a person. You know that, don't you."

"I do now," I said, feeling sick.

"He is real, though. He's a feeling people have in their hearts."

"Mom already told me that. It doesn't make sense to me."

"You see? That's the same problem a mother and father had a long time ago. They wanted to explain the Spirit of Giving to their own little girl, and they weren't having much luck at it. So they made up a story, a wonderful story about a fat, bearded fellow who loved to give presents, especially to children."

"Santa?"

"Yes. That little girl liked the story so well, she told it to her friends. Pretty soon, it spread around her whole neighborhood."

"But it was just a story," I said sadly.

Uncle Fritz nodded. "Yes. But that year, some parents gave their children presents with tags that said, 'From Santa.'"

"Then all the presents that come from Santa are really from parents?"

"From parents or from other people

who like you."

That wasn't as comforting as Uncle Fritz had meant it to be, for something unsettling had occurred to me. "What about the kids who don't have parents?" I asked. "Or what if the parents don't have any money? Then the kids don't get anything, do they?" My voice trembled on the last words, and my eyes were getting blurry with tears.

Uncle Fritz pulled me onto his lap. "You're growing up pretty fast, young one. You've put your finger right on the problem. There are kids right now who are waiting and hoping for him to come tonight, but their folks don't have anything to wrap up pretty and put under the tree. Unless someone else gives them some presents, they'll have a sad Christmas morning. Whoever helps out a family like that is the real Santa, whether he's dressed up in a red suit or not."

"Then do it, so you'll be the real Santa."

Uncle Fritz sat very still for a long time, like he was thinking. Then he said in a funny voice, "You're right." "I'm going to change clothes so I can go into town. If you want to come with me, you'd better get dressed."

"What are we going to do?"

"Buy some presents for a family down the road who needs to have a visit from Santa but won't—unless we do something about it."

"Good!" I said, reaching for my pants.

Uncle Fritz knew the kids in the family and had a good idea what they might like, but still he asked my opinion about toys as we walked up and down the crowded Ben Franklin aisles. We finally settled on a teddy bear and a pull toy for the family's little boy. For the girl we bought a doll and tea set. A game board was meant for the whole family.

I thought that was plenty, but Uncle Fritz had one more stop in mind. The grocery store.

"Who wants groceries for Christmas?" I said doubtfully.

"Someone who doesn't have much to eat."

I couldn't very well imagine what that would be like, but while Uncle Fritz put things like oatmeal and a ham in the shopping cart, I loaded it down with my favorite foods: peanut butter, candy bars, potato chips, raisins in little boxes, graham crackers, and sugared cereal. I wanted to give them some ice cream, too, but first I had to ask Uncle Fritz a question.

"Will they find the presents before ice cream would have a chance to melt?"

Uncle Fritz chuckled. "You're in Minnesota. Ice cream wouldn't melt even if they didn't find it until March."

So I added peppermint bonbon ice cream to the cart.

It was hard to keep my brothers and sister out of our surprise once they realized what was going on. "Get away from those things," I yelled as they surrounded the table laden with our booty. "This is something just for me and Uncle Fritz to do."

But Uncle Fritz said, "Santa doesn't have mean feelings, Annie. Why don't we let everyone help us get the packages ready? Then you and I will take them over together."

That sounded fair. We wrapped the toys in pretty paper and stuck ribbons on the oatmeal box and the ham. Grandma added some jars of applesauce and things like that from her pantry, and I saw Dad put some money in an envelope. By the time we loaded up the car, I think they were all as excited as I was.

Uncle Fritz and I didn't have far to drive. We had been on the road only a few minutes when he said, "That's their house up the road. I'd better turn off the lights so they won't see us coming and spoil our surprise." It was pitch black with the lights off, but Uncle Fritz got us safely up to their gate. Then ever so carefully, he opened his door. I started to do the same, but he shook his head, "You stay here. I don't want them to find you frozen on their porch along with the ice cream."

That wasn't such a bad idea, I thought. I was holding myself to keep from shaking with the cold, and my teeth were chattering. As Uncle Fritz picked up his first load, my breath misted the windows. I rubbed a spot clear so I could see him as he made one silent trip after another. And it seemed to me that there never could be a more real Santa than the Santa who put our boxes full of presents on the sagging porch of the house down the road from Grandma's and Grandpa's.

That was the beginning of a special relationship between me and Uncle Fritz. He wrote me letters and I wrote back. He became my confidant, listening to everything I had to say about my teachers, my boyfriends, and what I wanted to do with my life without thinking he had to put in his two-bits worth—something my parents couldn't resist.

But as I was growing up, Uncle Fritz was growing old. The fall I was a senior in high school, relatives called to tell us that he had died.

The night before the funeral relatives and friends congregated in the farmhouse. It was an odd evening, sad and happy at the same time. We all cried some, and hugged each other, and said how we would miss Uncle Fritz. Then we started telling our favorite stories about him. When it was my turn, I told the story about my thumb-sucking days and how I learned there was no Santa Claus.

I was all right when I started out, but as I got toward the end I could feel the tears welling up, and I knew I was going to cry. The last words I spoke getting too choked up to continue became my tribute and my farewell: "I know who Santa Claus is. Santa Claus is Uncle Fritz."

Carroll Hofeling Morris is the author of The Broken Covenant, The Bonsai, Saddle Shoe Blues, *and* The Merry Go Round.

GENTLE JESUS

by Mabel Jones Gabbott

Gentle Jesus in the manger
Came to teach us all to care
For each other, for the stranger,
Came to show us love and prayer.

Gentle Jesus, Holy Baby
Born in little Bethlehem.
Shepherds brought their gifts to praise him.
Magi left him precious gems.

Gentle Jesus in the starlight,
Heav'nly angels sang his birth.
Gentle Jesus in the stable,
Lord of heav'n and Lord of earth.

WHEN LOVE CAME DOWN

by Mabel Jones Gabbott

The night was still, and then a song awakened shepherds 'round their fire,
And hastened them to Bethlehem! Hosannas from a heav'nly choir!

This was the night when Love came down, as promised in God's holy word.
The angels heralded in song the blessed birth of Christ, our Lord.

This was the night the King was born, as stars foretold in distant space;
And three who watched the skies were led to Bethlehem, that holy place.

This was the night when Love came down, as promised in God's holy word.
The angels heralded in song the blessed birth of Christ, our Lord.

This was the night, that holy night, when Love came down to bless the earth.
And men and angels worshipped Him this night, the night of Jesus' birth.

This was the night when Love came down, as promised in God's holy word.
The angels heralded in song the blessed birth of Christ, our Lord.

This was the birth of Christ, our Lord.

*Mabel Jones Gabbott is a former editorial associate on
the staffs of the* Improvement Era *and the* Ensign.
*She composed the hymn, "In Humility, Our Savior."
She is also the author of a children's book,* Heroes of
the Book of Mormon. *"Gentle Jesus" and "When
Love Came Down" are lyrics to music by Michael F.
Moody.*

CHRISTMAS BREADS

by Dora D. Flack

Bread is a year-round staff of life at our house, but at Christmastime fancy breads are special treats for family, guests, and neighbors.

Using detailed instructions, I hope to guide home bakers past possible mistakes and/or frustrations with the following recipes. For example, *mixer* in the basic recipe usually refers to a mixmaster, and the kneading must be finished by hand. A *breadmixer* shortens the whole process. But whether you use a mixer or knead by hand, breadmaking can be fun.

Cardamom Christmas Trees

Basic Holiday Dough Recipe

2 cups milk, scalded
2 tablespoons active dry yeast
3/4 cup granulated sugar
3/4 cup shortening
1 tablespoon salt
3 eggs, beaten
1 teaspoon cardamom (or substitute 1 teaspoon ginger or 2 teaspoons cinnamon or nutmeg)
about 6 to 7 cups all-purpose flour

In a medium-size saucepan, scald milk

(don't boil). Remove from burner and add sugar and shortening. Let cool to 120 degrees F. Stir and add yeast to dissolve. Sift 3 cups flour with salt and cardamom.

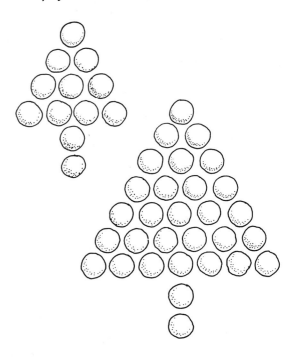

In a small mixing bowl beat eggs well. Pour eggs into large mixing bowl, adding yeast-milk mixture. Beat for 3 minutes on medium to high speed. With slotted spoon,

stir in flour until stiff enough to turn out onto floured breadboard or pastry cloth. Knead, gradually adding flour until a soft, elastic ball is formed. Return dough to mixer bowl and let rise until double in bulk. Punch down and let rise a second time.

For large trees, grease 2 large cookie sheets. Only a large 17 x 14-inch sheet will accommodate 30 balls for a big tree. Turn out dough onto lightly oiled formica table or countertop. Divide dough in half. From each half (for big tree) form 30 balls, 1 1/2 inches round. Cutting dough with a pizza cutter ensures uniformity. Cup oiled palms of both hands and work dough (under each palm) over oiled surface, forming smooth balls. Use oil sparingly. Practice makes perfect with this step. You may prefer to use a floured surface for making balls.

Building the tree. Near the bottom of the cookie sheet, and in the middle of the width, place 2 balls, one above the other, for the trunk. Now proceed to build the tree. Place the balls barely apart to allow for rising.

Cover loosely with plastic wrap and let rise until double in bulk, usually about 30 to 45 minutes, depending on room temperature. Carefully remove plastic wrap and bake on bottom rack of preheated oven at 375 to 400 degrees F. for 12 to 15 minutes, or until golden brown. Remove from oven and let stand in pan 5 to 10 minutes. Very carefully remove with a spatula to serving tray. An open-ended cookie sheet is helpful.

Frost with butter icing. Decorate as desired with colored sugar or multicolored balls or with candied fruits for "ornaments."

This bread is superb when eaten fresh. Leftovers can be reheated in microwave oven; 20-30 seconds only will not completely melt frosting, and balls simulate "oven freshness."

Butter Icing

3 cups powdered sugar
1/4 cup butter
4 tablespoons plus 1 teaspoon evaporated milk

In medium-size mixing bowl, combine ingredients and beat well. This will ice 2 large trees. Drizzle the icing and decorate with red and green glazed cherries.

If tree is not to be served almost immediately, cover with a towel. Plastic wrap causes sweating. If freezing trees for later use, wrap well in plastic wrap or aluminum foil, then ice and decorate when thawed.

Tip for trees. Make trees any desired size down to 3 balls across the bottom row above the trunk, with one ball for the trunk. This tiny tree requires only 7 balls.

Ladder Roll

The Basic Holiday Dough recipe makes 4 Ladder Rolls. Roll a quarter portion into an oblong 15 x 6 inches either on floured board or an oiled surface. Place rolled dough on a greased cookie sheet.

Choose a filling and spoon it down the center, leaving a good 1 1/2 inches of uncovered dough on each side. With scissors, about every 2 inches down the length of the oblong dough, cut from the edge of the dough toward the filling. Make 7 or 8 cuts on each side along the whole length of the oblong. Bring matching strips of dough from opposite sides to the center, crossing strips over the filling.

Let rise as with Christmas trees. Bake at 350 to 375 degrees F. for approximately 25 minutes. To avoid excessive top browning, slip a sheet of aluminum foil on top of roll during last half of baking.

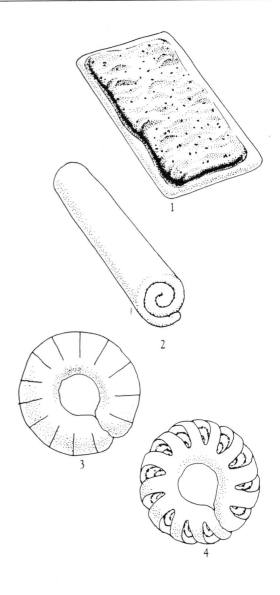

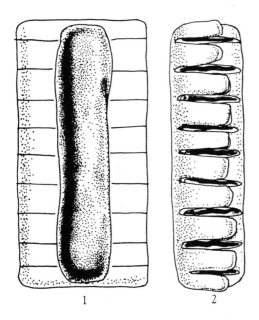

Swedish Tea Ring

The Basic Holiday Dough recipe makes 3 or 4 Swedish Tea Rings. Choose and prepare a filling. Roll out the oblong of dough and spread with filling. Roll as for a jelly roll and form into a ring. Place on greased cookie sheet.

With scissors, cut from the outer edge toward the center, halfway through. Twist the little cut half-slices upward so that the filling shows. If desired, a maraschino or candied cherry can be placed in each upturned half circle. Let rise as with Christmas Trees.

Bake at 350 to 375 degrees F. about 25 minutes. To avoid excessive browning on top, slip a sheet of aluminum foil over the rings during last half of baking time.

Let stand 5-10 minutes before removing to serving tray.

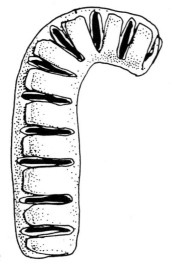

Candy Cane

The Basic Holiday Dough recipe makes 3 or 4 Candy Canes. Divide dough into 3 or 4 portions, as desired. Proceed as if making a Ladder Roll, using canned cherry pie filling. Gently turn the top of the roll to resemble the curve of a candy cane. Let rise as with Christmas Trees.

Bake at 350 to 375 degrees F. about 25 minutes. To avoid excessive browning on top, slip a sheet of aluminum foil over the canes during last half of baking time.

This roll can be frosted, but I prefer lightly sifting powdered sugar over it or leaving it plain. Or decorate with candied fruit.

Tip. Use portions of Holiday Bread Dough for a variety of Christmas breads. This dough is superb for any type of roll, as well as the ones given here. For additional flavor, substitute half of flour with whole wheat flour.

Dora D. Flack is the author or coauthor of Gifts Only You Can Give, Wheat for Man, Fun with Fruit Preservation, Dry and Save, Preserving Your Past, Christmas Magic, Bread Baking Made Easy, and England's First Convert, among others.

THE SQUASH-BLOSSOM NECKLACE

by Blaine M. and Brenton G. Yorgason

The old stairs groaned loudly as David Michael Teague slowly descended them. Without even looking he knew that the ancient clock on the wall showed ten minutes past eight, and that meant he was ten minutes late opening up. Somehow, though, it just didn't seem to matter. In fact, it was getting hard to make anything really matter anymore.

At the foot of the stairs he paused to survey the long narrow room before him. Through the twilight of the still-drawn shades he let his eyes drift over the shelves, the half-empty shelves that held the sum total of his worldly goods.

A moment only he stood thus, for the prospects those shelves revealed were so discouraging that he could only think about them for a few moments without becoming terribly depressed, and David Michael Teague simply would not allow himself that fatal luxury. If he had little else, he at least had peace of mind knowing that he was his own boss and was doing his best. It might not be that significant, but it was his best.

Quickly he ran a stanza of his favorite hymn, "The Day Dawn Is Breaking," through his mind. That hymn always made him smile, and as it did so once again he walked briskly to the front of the store to pull the shades and open the door to another and, he hoped, better day.

Sixty-seven dollars and eighteen cents! The grand total of yesterday's gross receipts. It was a good thing the rent on the old building was so low, and it was a good thing too that he could live in the room upstairs. He surely couldn't afford to live anywhere else.

He thought back to his mission for the Church a dozen years before. Funny, but it didn't seem that long ago. His mission had been wonderful, but at the time it had seemed to last forever. Now he had been home six times that long and he wondered where the years had gone.

Anyway, he could think of apartments he had lived in near the reservation that had seemed luxurious compared to his room upstairs. Still, the room was warm and the bed was soft, and what more could a man ask for?

At the window he leaned over to grasp the pull on the shade, and as he did so he saw again the necklace placed carefully in the center of his window display. Halting then he stood for a moment gazing at it.

How that necklace stirred the depths of his soul! It was Apache silver and turquoise, delicately shaped in a squash-blossom pattern, and it was truly the most beautiful necklace he had ever seen.

He thought back to when, as a missionary, he had first met the old Apache who was, as he explained it, guardian of the necklace. Though knowing of the necklace, and being deeply moved by its beauty, Elder Teague had refrained from speaking of it to the old man for several weeks. While impatient by nature, he had learned the value of the Apache way, the way of deliberate slowness and thoughtful care. The necklace, he knew, had taken someone months to create. It was not something that he would wish to discuss immediately.

At last, however, the proper moment arrived. It was late, both he and his companion were seated cross-legged on blankets, and across the fire the old man sat silently, his necklace seeming to dance in the light of the fire.

Cautiously Elder Teague inquired about the necklace. After an appropriate moment of silence, the old man quietly spoke.

"*She-ke-sin,* my young friend, at last it comes. You are truly becoming one with the people. I have seen your eyes glowing with eagerness like the stars are glowing in the star nations above. This Apache warrior congratulates you for the patience you have shown."

"Thank you, my friend," Elder Teague replied.

"But you have asked of the necklace, *She-ke-sin,* and I will tell you what I know. The necklace is old, much older than my grandfather. It has a life of its own, and a name. It is called *Yenta,* which, to the Apache, means matchmaker. Whether the necklace itself is Apache, this man does not know. It came to me as a youth. The wise one who hung it upon my shoulders prophesied that it would lead me to my *She-ah,* my wife, and that the necklace would bring peace to our lodge always. This it has done."

After months of close friendship with the old man, Elder Teague received his mission release. On the eve of his departure, knowing that he would likely never see his old friend again, he and his companion drove out to say good-bye.

Following a pleasant though emotional visit, Elder Teague stood to go. For a moment he and the old man clasped hands, and then with a sudden movement the old man removed the necklace and draped it around the neck of Elder Teague.

"My son," he said quietly, "this old man gives you *Yenta,* for thus the Spirit has directed. Treasure and protect it, and it will lead you to your *She-ah,* the one *Yenta* would have you find happi-

ness with—one whose eyes are the color of these stones. Now go quickly, my son, in peace."

For over twelve years David had kept that necklace close to him, yet in all that time there had never been a girl with sky-blue eyes, nor a girl with any other color of eyes, for that matter. David Michael Teague was as alone today, if not more so, than he had been the day he was released from his missionary labors. *Yenta* had simply not worked.

Sixty-seven dollars and eighteen cents! What meager receipts for a shopping day just two days before Christmas. And that was why the necklace was in the window. David was broke, his rent long overdue. The necklace the old Apache had given him was the most valuable as well as the most beautiful item in his possession, and despite his own personal feelings about it, he desperately needed the money that its sale could bring. So now it was in the window, and when it was sold he would also sell a part of himself, the part that was wrapped around the sacred dream, which the old Indian had given him, of the girl with the sky-blue eyes.

As he reached down and pulled the shade, he was almost startled to see the small nose pressed against the fogged-up window pane. Almost, but not quite, for this was the third morning the little fellow had been standing there, waiting for the shades to be drawn so that he could see the necklace.

David unlocked the door and then walked behind the counter, anxiously considering how much he was counting on the sale of that necklace. It was almost humorous, too, especially when one considered that so far the only person who had shown any interest in the necklace was the little boy out front.

The day went fast, much faster than usual, for last-minute shoppers were scurrying around looking for the unusual or hard-to-find items that David seemed to have an affinity for when he went on his rare buying trips.

So it was a pretty good day as far as his days went, and he was satisfied, as he prepared to close the store, that his day's receipts would top a hundred dollars. Yes, and even more important, an elderly lady, with a dog that bore a remarkable resemblance to her, had been in the store and had expressed great interest in his squash-blossom necklace. She had promised that she would be in tomorrow to tell him whether or not she would give him his desired price for it. What a Christmas present that would make for him! Why, with seven hundred dollars. . . .

The ringing of the bell above the door brought David's thoughts back to earth, and when he looked down he saw, standing across the counter looking up at him, the little boy who had stood at the window the three days previous.

"Hi," David said, smiling at the little guy whose eyes were not even level with the countertop. "May I help you?"

"Uh-huh. I wanna buy a necklace."

"A necklace, huh. Well, good! We have some very pretty necklaces here in this box, and you just tell me which one you want. This one is very pretty, and . . ."

"No, them ain't the ones. I want the one with the pretty blue rocks."

"Blue rocks?" asked David, already knowing what the child wanted.

"Yeah," the boy beamed, "it's for Sissie."

David's head whirled with a dozen questions, chief among them being who this little boy might be. He surely couldn't have that kind of money, but then one never knew. Maybe he could. But no . . . there was no way that . . . Still, what harm could it do to show him the necklace up close, and then explain to him how valuable it was and that it was simply too expensive for him to buy.

Carefully David took the necklace from the window and placed it on the counter before the little boy, who stood motionless gazing at it for a long moment. Then, with a smile creeping across his face, he carefully stretched out one finger and gently caressed one of the smaller stones.

"Yep," he said happily, "that's the one, all right."

"It's pretty, isn't it," David said softly.

"Yep, real pretty."

"And expensive, too," David added, doing his best to make the word *expensive* sound significant to the child.

"Oh yeah," the boy sighed, "but I've got the money home on my

dresser . . . all my nickels and dimes and quarters. I'll be back tomorrow to get it."

With that, the boy was gone, and David, smiling wistfully, picked up the necklace.

"*She-ke-sin,*" he thought suddenly. "I wonder what my old Apache friend would say if he knew I was trying to sell his necklace. If he knew my circumstances, I'm sure he would understand."

The next day, the last one before Christmas, was another slow one, and in the whole day he didn't turn over eighty dollars. Or he didn't until the lady with the matching dog came in and paid him the full seven hundred dollars he'd asked for the necklace. As David lifted it from the window and began wrapping it, he felt a strange tightening in his chest, and he saw before him, not the woman and the dog, but an old Apache Indian smiling at him across the flickering tongues of a small campfire.

"There you are, ma'am," he said emotionally. "I do hope you have a merry Christmas."

"Oh, I will," the woman beamed. "This will look so lovely. Thank you, son, and merry Christmas to you."

The last two hours of business dragged slowly, and it was just at closing time that the little boy came bursting through the door.

"I got the money, mister! You got my necklace wrapped?"

"I . . . a . . . well, son, I sold the necklace already."

"You . . . sold my necklace? But you couldn't! I told you yesterday I wanted it for Sissie, and here's my money right here in my handkerchief."

As the little boy held up his handkerchief with the coins knotted inside, David saw that he was starting to cry.

"I'm sorry, son," David said simply, not knowing what else to do.

With a soft wail, the boy turned and ran from the shop. Already feeling terrible, David watched with mounting horror as the child darted into the path of an oncoming truck.

There was a screeching of tires, and in an instant David was kneeling beside the still and bleeding form of the child who still clutched tightly the knotted handkerchief.

In a matter of minutes the ambulance carrying David and the boy arrived at the hospital. As the stretcher bearing the boy was rolled into the emergency room, David found himself being ushered to an office, where he began the frustrating process of admitting the boy.

"I don't know his name," David said for the third time. "He was just a customer in my store. Can't we ask him?"

"I'm sorry, sir, but as we have explained, he is unconscious . . . and a child must be signed in by a responsible adult. You'll have to sign for him, sir, and be financially responsible for his stay here."

Sensing the futility of argument, and hoping the boy's parents would pay the bill, he signed. As he did so, he smiled wryly, thinking that with his luck the boy would be an orphan and he would end up paying anyway. It would serve him right for selling the necklace in the first place.

It was two hours before the doctors came to the waiting room to discuss the boy's serious but stable condition. After the doctors had gone, David went to the boy's room and waited, hoping that the child soon would regain consciousness so that David could notify his family.

Early the next morning, as David was dozing in the chair, the door beside him quietly opened, and he found himself gazing into the bluest eyes he had ever seen.

"Bobby, is that you? Bobby, answer me . . . are you all right?"

Running to the bed, the young woman cradled the boy's head in her shaking arms. "Oh, Bobby," she said. "Please. Not you, too. You can't leave me here alone."

"Excuse me, ma'am," David said softly.

The woman turned, and through tear-filled eyes she questioned, "Who are you? And what are you doing here with Bobby?"

"I'm David Teague, ma'am. Bobby was in my store and I saw the whole thing. We didn't know your son's name, so there was no way we could contact you or your husband. He was in my store to buy a present for his little sister, but I had . . ."

At that moment Bobby coughed and opened his eyes, and the woman, holding him close, broke into tears again, sobbing his name over and over.

Feeling decidedly uncomfortable, David was turning toward the door when the boy spoke.

"Sissie," he said, his voice sounding tiny and faraway, "I was going to get you a present, but the man already sold it, and I didn't get you nothing."

"Hush, Bobby. It's okay. I . . . "

"Sissie?" David asked startled. "Did he call you Sissie?"

"Yes," she said, "of course he did. I'm his sister."

"But . . . but . . . I thought . . . well, I expected . . . but you're not little! And you're not his mother?"

"Well . . . I have been his mother since Mom and Dad died. But really, I'm just his sister."

David could not get over the woman's eyes. Her hair was auburn, framing a delicate yet bold oval face . . . but her eyes, her blue, blue eyes. Wistfully, David thought of the necklace, his squash-blossom necklace. The stones were the color of her eyes. "Oh," he groaned inwardly, "if only I hadn't sold . . . "

"But Sissie," Bobby said, interrupting David's erstwhile thoughts. "What about Christmas? What am I going to get you for Christmas?"

"Bobby, you don't have to get me anything. I've had a wonderful Christmas already. Just look at what my boss, Mrs. Hrebicek, gave me. She said that after five years I had earned this. Isn't it beautiful!"

And David Michael Teague stared in amazement as the woman quickly unwrapped her scarf and opened her coat, revealing *Yenta,* the matchmaker. David's squash-blossom necklace.

Blaine M. and Brenton G. Yorgason are among the most widely read LDS authors. Their collective works include Brother Brigham's Gold, Becoming, The Loftier Way, The Shadow Taker, The Greatest Quest, Seven Days for Ruby, In Search of Steenie Bergman, Charlie's Monument, The Windwalker, *and* The Bishop's Horse Race.

A CELEBRATION OF CHRISTMAS

by Richard and Marilynne Linford

This script may be presented as a home evening, a readers' theatre, a play, or a pageant. Many special effects can be added to enhance the evening. You may wish to consider the following:

1. Those who plan to attend could come dressed in a costume of the time of Christ.

2. Food similar to that eaten at the time of Christ—bread, fruit, stew, olives, figs, and grape juice—could be served. Guests could recline on mats and pillows instead of using chairs and tables.

3. Those attending could bring a gift to exchange that evening or to be given to the needy later.

4. Each individual or family could come with a flashlight, if distances permit, and walk from their homes to the meeting place, everyone leaving at a specified time. The effect of seeing many lights converging on the meeting place is moving.

5. If the pageant is outdoors, live animals could be used. (A live nativity at the Washington, D.C. Temple helped

draw hundreds of thousands of visitors.)

6. Musical numbers could be performed by a choir in the back of the room or hall.

7. A program could be printed detailing the sequence of events including words to the music.

8. Segments could be prerecorded. Sound effects could be added.

9. If you think Christmas carols would increase spirituality before the play begins, three appropriate hymns are: "Oh, Come, All Ye Faithful"; "It Came upon the Midnight Clear"; and "O Little Town of Bethlehem."

Scene 1:

Narrator: For our story this evening, the stage (room) is divided in half. The left half is set as a living area in the home of the Book of Mormon prophet Nephi III, son of Nephi, grandson of Helaman, in the New World city of Bountiful in the ninety-first year of the reign of the judges. The right half is set as a bedroom in Nazareth several months before the birth of Jesus Christ.

Our story begins on the Bountiful

side of the stage. A ten-year-old girl, Sarah, is doing some embroidery. Her mother, Rebecca, sits in a chair, her embroidery in her lap, her complete attention on a scene outside her living room window.

Sarah: (Holding up her sampler) Look, Mother. I have finished the gold in the sun.

Rebecca: (Keeping her attention on the scene outside) Yes, that's nice, Sarah.

Sarah: Doesn't it look real with all the oranges and yellows, and now this bit of gold here and there?

Rebecca: Yes, dear.

Sarah: Mother, what is wrong? You are usually so interested in my embroidery. We have heard Samuel the Lamanite on the wall prophesying for many days. Why are you listening so hard today?

Rebecca: Come sit here beside me and you will see how angry some of our people are. Your father has tried for so long to call them to repentance, and many refuse to listen. It just shows how wicked the Nephites have become when the Lord sends a Lamanite prophet to prophesy to us, when usually it has been the Nephite prophets who have been sent to the Lamanites. Oh, no! Look at that group of people coming down the hill!

Sarah: Mother, what shall we do? They have bows and arrows and bags of stones. They are going to hurt Samuel!

Rebecca: They are throwing stones at him, but he seems unconcerned. How I admire him! He speaks with even more boldness. Look! The Lord is protecting him. The stones all miss him. Listen!

Samuel the Lamanite's voice: Behold, I give unto you a sign; for five years more cometh, and behold, then cometh the Son of God to redeem all those who shall believe on his name. And behold, this will I give unto you for a sign at the time of his coming; for behold, there shall be great lights in the heaven, insomuch that in the night before he cometh there shall be no darkness, insomuch that it shall appear unto man as if it was day.

Therefore, there shall be one day and a night and a day, as if it were one day and there were no night; and this shall be unto you for a sign; for ye shall know of the rising of the sun and also of its setting; therefore they shall know of a surety that there shall be two days and a night; nevertheless the night shall not be darkened; and it shall be the night before he is born. And behold, there shall a new star arise, such an one as ye never have beheld; and this also shall be a sign unto you.

Rebecca: Did you hear, Sarah? In five years the Son of God will be born. Now surely the people will repent when they realize the time is so soon.

Sarah: I will be fifteen when he is born. How will it be to have a night when it isn't dark and there will be a great new star? Isn't it exciting, Mother!

(Nephi enters.)

Rebecca: Oh, Nephi! They are throwing stones at Samuel. Others carry bows and arrows. Is that what brings you home at this time of the day?

Nephi: (Putting his arms around his wife to comfort her) Yes. I have been so busy baptizing those who have been touched by Samuel's words that I have failed to think enough about Samuel's safety. Last night we talked again and together planned for his escape back to his own land if the crowd should become violent. The Lord will allow him to finish his message today and then he will be gone to preach and prophesy among his own people.

Sarah: (She has stayed by the window) Father, Father, look. They realize that their stones don't hit him, so they are using arrows. The people are calling to their captains.

Voice 1: Take this fellow and bind him, for behold he hath a devil.

Voice 2: Because of the devil which is in him, we cannot hit him with our stones and our arrows.

Voice 3: Let's take him and bind him.

Many voices: Away with him. Away with him.

Nephi: There, he gives me the signal we agreed upon. I must go and help him escape.

Rebecca: Be careful. May God be with you.

Samuel's voice: And now behold, saith the Lord, concerning the people of the Nephites: If they will not repent, and observe to do my will, I will utterly destroy them.

Sarah: Mother, those men are climbing up the wall towards Samuel. Look, they are running after him. I am so afraid for Samuel and Father.

Rebecca: (Comforting Sarah) Don't worry. God sent him to us, and God will protect Samuel and your father.

Scene 2:

(The Bountiful side of the stage dims and the Nazareth side is lighted. A young woman, Mary, is in her bedroom preparing for sleep.)

Mary: How fortunate I am! I am to be married to Joseph—the most tender and handsome and righteous man, and also the best young carpenter, in all of Judea. I sing praises to the Lord for His goodness to me.

(The room begins to grow lighter and lighter. Mary's surprise turns to apprehension and then fear. As the light grows more intense, an angel is seen.)

Gabriel: Mary, you are highly favored by Heavenly Father. You are most blessed among all women.

Mary: Who are you? Why would you come to me? Why do you greet me with those words?

Gabriel: My name is Gabriel. I am sent from the presence of God, so do not be afraid, Mary, for you have found favor with God.

Mary: Is there something that I should do that I'm not doing? Just tell me and I will do it.

Gabriel: Mary, God has chosen you to be the mother of his Only Begotten Son in the flesh. A son will be born to you and you shall name him Jesus. He shall be great and shall be called the Son of the highest, and the Lord God shall give Him the throne of His father David; and He shall reign over the house of Jacob forever; and of His kingdom there shall be no end.

Mary: How can this happen? I am not married. I am a virgin.

Gabriel: Mary, the Holy Ghost shall come to thee and the power of the highest shall overshadow thee, and you will give birth to the Son of God.

Mary: I have often thought in my heart how blessed the woman would be who would be chosen to be the mother of the Messiah. I am honored by this message you bring. I am the Lord's servant and my soul glorifies the Lord. May it be to me as you have said.

Gabriel: Your cousin Elizabeth who is old and has never been able to have a child will give birth to a son in three months. This child will be the one who will help prepare the people for the coming of the Lord. Go visit Elizabeth and rejoice with her. Farewell, Mary.

Scene 3:

(The light fades, and as Gabriel leaves, Mary kneels beside her bed in prayer and thanksgiving. The lights on the other side of the stage are brought up to show Nephi sitting at his desk engraving on the gold plates. He is speaking to his wife as he writes.)

Nephi: A great division is taking place among our people.

Rebecca: Yes, I know. With so many signs and wonders, well, miracles, the good are getting better—

Nephi: And the bad are getting worse. Today the leader of the opposition and his followers set a date. If the signs prophesied by Samuel do not happen by then, they say they will kill all of us. They make a great uproar throughout the land. They say the time is past, and that our joy and faith concerning this thing are in vain.

Rebecca: They have set an exact date?

Nephi: Yes. It is a few months away. But I fear that the unbelievers have set a time that is too soon, and I worry lest by any means all those who believe in Samuel's prophecies should be put to death.

Scene 4:

(Lights dim on the Bountiful side and go up on the Nazareth side to show a young man, Joseph, on his knees in prayer.)

Joseph: Oh, my Father. What shall I do? I am engaged to Mary. I know she is going to have a baby. Thou knowest that I am a just man and not willing to embarrass her or allow the people to harm her. Shall I send her away secretly or what? I love and want to do thy will. Help me please to know thy desire.

(Joseph gets up from his prayer and lies down on his bed. The angel Gabriel is seen behind a brightly lighted veil. He speaks to Joseph.)

Gabriel: Joseph, Joseph, son of David. Don't be afraid to take Mary to be your wife. The child she is going to have is the Son of God. You are a greatly loved son of your Father, and He has chosen you to protect, love and teach His son, the Messiah, the Savior of the world, while He is a child on earth. Go for-ward, Joseph. This is the will of the Lord to you.

(Gabriel departs and the scene quickly changes. Mary and Joseph are traveling to Bethlehem.)

Joseph: You are strong, Mary, to travel this way with the baby due at any time.

Mary: I am blessed, Joseph. The prophecies say the Christ Child will be born in Bethlehem, the home of our royal fathers. Only God could have brought us to Bethlehem at this precise time. But Joseph, I do feel the time of birth is getting close. Oh, Joseph, I love you.

Joseph: I love you too, Mary. The decree from Caesar Augustus that all the world should be taxed has brought us to Bethlehem, city of David, our ancestor, just when the baby is ready to come. Mary, even though you are weary from the travel and big with child, you are still beautiful. I am honored to be your husband. I pray that we will quickly find a place for the night.

Scene 5:

(The lights dim on the Bethlehem side and the lights on the Bountiful side are brought up to show Nephi seated at a table. His wife stands next to him, her hand on his back, consoling him.)

Nephi: What am I to do? The Lord has called me to be a prophet to this people. Five years ago He even sent Samuel as another witness to help me warn the people to repent. The unrighteous so outnumber the humble members of the Church, and now there is a threat to kill all who believe that Samuel's words will be fulfilled. If Samuel's words are not fulfilled this very day, we will all be put to death, including our beloved children. My heart is weary. What if we are one day off in our calculation of when the five years are ended? There will be none of the righteous to see the fulfillment of Samuel's prophecy.

Rebecca: Nephi, I have been visiting the members all day today. In every home they are fasting and praying as you requested. Even the little children are fasting. The Lord will hear our pleading. He protected Samuel on the wall and allowed him to escape. He will provide a way for us to escape.

Nephi: Yes, I have faith that he will. I will go with you to visit more of the members in a little while. Please leave me here with my thoughts for just a while.

(Nephi's wife goes offstage. Nephi falls to his knees and cries mightily in prayer.)

Nephi: Father, thou who brought Lehi to this promised land, thou who made the prison walls to crumble to save my father Nephi from the hands of the Lamanites, thou who watches over thy children day and night, hear thy servant's prayer. Those who believe in thee and in the words of thy prophet Samuel are in great danger. As thou knowest, the enemies of the Church have set today as the deadline. If the signs Samuel prophesied of are not given tonight, they will kill all faithful members. Father, as thou knowest, all of the members with their children are fasting and praying today that thou wilt in thine own way preserve us and provide a way that we may live. Nevertheless, thy will be done.

Voice of the Lord: Nephi, Nephi. Lift up your head and be of good cheer; for behold, the time is at hand, and on this night shall the sign be given, and on the morrow come I into the world, to show unto the world that I will fulfill all that which I have caused to be spoken by the mouth of my holy prophets. . . . And behold, the time is at hand, and this night shall the sign be given.

Narrator: And it came to pass that the words which came unto the Book of Mormon prophet Nephi were fulfilled, according as they had been spoken; for behold, at the going down of the sun there was no darkness; and the people began to be astonished because there was no darkness when the night came.

And there were many, who had not believed the words of the prophets, who fell to the earth and became as if they were dead, for they knew that the great plan of destruction which they had laid for those who believed in the words of the prophets had been frustrated; for the sign which had been given was already at hand.

And it came to pass that there was no darkness in all that night; but it was as light as though it was mid-day. And it came to pass that the sun did rise in the morning again, according to its proper order; and they knew that it was the day that the Lord should be born. . . . And it came to pass also that a new star did appear.

Scene 6:

(Lights dim on the Bountiful scene and raise on Bethlehem. A giant star is now illuminated directly over the middle of the stage. Mary is resting. The baby Jesus is wrapped in swaddling clothes near her. Joseph is standing nearby. The choir or congregation hums one verse of "Away in a Manger," and sings the other verses. Choir and or congregation sings "Once in Royal David's City.")

Mary: I am so tired yet so thankful that Jesus is born. I give God great thanks, Joseph. I am also grateful for you, Joseph. You have been gentle, thoughtful, and kind. Thank you for being such a wonderful husband.

Joseph: Mary, you deserve the praise. I have heard about women in childbirth, and you were a queen.

Mary: I had to be brave, Joseph, for as you know, this babe in my arms is

the King and Messiah. See how beautiful He is.

(The choir or congregation sings "For Unto Us a Child Is Born" from Handel's *Messiah.*)

(From the far side of the stage out of the audience a group of shepherds stands and looks toward the stage.)

(Choir and congregation sing "Far, Far Away on Judea's Plains.")

(If a pageant is being presented the following music may be added here: Soprano and choir or congregation sing Recitative for Soprano, "There Were Shepherds Abiding in the Field"; Recitative for Soprano, "And Lo! The Angel of the Lord Came Upon Them"; No. 16, Recitative for Soprano, "And Suddenly There Was with the Angel"; and No. 17, Chorus, "Glory to God," all from Handel's *Messiah.*)

Shepherd 1: This is a night of all nights. We have been visited by angels. A new star shines in the heavens. And we search in the city of David for the Savior who is Christ the Lord. Look! A stable. This may be the place.

Shepherd 2: The angel said we should find the babe wrapped in swaddling clothes and lying in a manger.

Shepherd 3: He is here! Come and see the Christ Child who the heavenly choir sang would bring "Peace on earth, goodwill toward men."

(Shepherds enter the stable and kneel before the babe. Choir and/or congregation sing "Angels We Have Heard on High," and "Joy to the World.")

Scene 7:

(The lights again focus on Nephi's home.)

Sarah: Here we are, Father; what did you want?

Nephi: I know you are out looking at the amazing star that shines brightly even though it is midday, but I want to read a scripture to you.

Sarah: Is it about the Christ Child?

Nephi: Rebecca, can you join us for a few minutes?

(Rebecca comes to hear as Nephi reads.)

Nephi: Yes, Sarah. The scriptures are full of prophecies concerning the birth of Jesus Christ. Let me read to you first from the small plates which were written by the first Nephi, the son of Lehi. Sarah, as I read the words he wrote of a vision he had, imagine in your mind the same thing. We are here in the Promised Land, thousands of miles

from the birthplace of the Lord, but we still can enjoy this blessed time even as do those who are there. Listen to the words of Nephi, a prophet of God, written almost six hundred years ago.

"And I beheld the city of Nazareth; and in the city of Nazareth I beheld a virgin, and she was exceedingly fair and white. . . . [And the angel said she was to be the mother of the Son of God.] And it came to pass that I beheld that she was carried away in the Spirit; and after . . . a space of time the angel spake unto me, saying: Look!

"And I looked and beheld the virgin again, bearing a child in her arms. And the angel said unto me: Behold the Lamb of God, yea, even the Son of the Eternal Father!" (Lights begin to dim.) And then from the Brass Plates the prophecies of Isaiah: "For unto us a child is born, unto us a son is given; and the government shall be upon his shoulder; and his name shall be called, Wonderful, Counselor, The Mighty God, The Everlasting Father, The Prince of Peace."

(Choir and/or congregation sings "Hallelujah!" from Handel's *Messiah*. Congregation then sings "Silent Night.")

Richard and Marilynne Linford coauthored the book I Hope They Call Me On a Mission Too! *Marilynne is the author of* Is Anyone Out There Building Mother's Self-Esteem?

FAVORITE HOLIDAY FARE

by Winnifred C. Jardine

Baked Halibut with Tartar Sauce

4 halibut fillets (about 1 1/2 pounds)
4 tablespoons (1/2 stick) butter, melted
1/2 small onion, finely grated
2 tablespoons fresh lemon juice
Paprika
Chopped fresh parsley or cilantro
Tartar Sauce (see below)

Preheat oven to 450 degrees F. Melt butter in baking pan large enough to hold fillets. Dip fillets in melted butter, turning to coat all sides. Spread grated onion evenly over each fillet; squeeze fresh lemon juice over top and sprinkle liberally with paprika. (This may be done ahead of time and refrigerated; remove 1/2 hour before baking.) Bake in preheated oven, allowing 12 minutes of cooking time for each 1 inch of thickness in fillets. When done, fish will flake at thickest portion. Sprinkle with chopped fresh parsley or cilantro and paprika. Serve immediately with tartar sauce. Makes 4 servings.

Tartar Sauce:

1 cup mayonnaise (may use part plain yogurt)
1 tablespoon capers, drained and chopped fine

1 teaspoon Dijon mustard
2 tablespoons finely chopped sweet gherkin pickles
2 teaspoons lemon juice
1/2 teaspoon grated onion
2 tablespoons chopped parsley

In mixing bowl thoroughly combine all ingredients. Cover and store in refrigerator. Serve at room temperature. Makes 1 1/4 cups.

Crisscross Salad

2 stalks (1 to 1 1/2 pounds) fresh broccoli
1/2 red onion
2 tomatoes, seeded and diced
1 cup (4 oz.) medium to sharp Cheddar cheese, coarsely grated
1 can (8 oz.) red kidney beans, drained
2/3 cup hot Italian dressing (see below)

Clean broccoli and dice into pieces about size of kidney bean. Toss with remaining ingredients until all vegetables are thoroughly coated with dressing. Cover and refrigerate 24 hours. Makes 8-12 servings.

Hot Italian Dressing:

1/2 teaspoon salt
1/4 teaspoon ground pepper
1/4 teaspoon celery salt

1/8 teaspoon mustard
Dash Tabasco sauce
1 small clove garlic, minced
2 tablespoons salad vinegar
1/2 cup salad oil

In jar combine all ingredients. Cover and shake vigorously. Makes 2/3 cup.

Cranberry Mint Cheesecake

This should be made 2 days before serving.

Crust:
1/4 pound (1 stick) butter
2 cups very finely ground crumbs from Nabisco Nilla Wafers
1/4 cup sugar

Melt butter over lowest heat. Combine butter with crumbs and sugar in food processor or blender until well blended (or combine in plastic container with fork). Press mixture over bottom and up sides of ungreased 10-inch springform pan.

Filling:
2 pounds (4 8-ounce packages) cream cheese
1 1/2 cups sugar
1 1/2 tablespoons mint extract
Pinch salt
4 large eggs
2 cups fresh cranberries

Preheat oven to 350 degrees F. In mixer combine cream cheese and sugar and beat for 2 minutes until soft (cream cheese need not be at room temperature). Add mint extract and salt; blend thoroughly. Eggs need not be at room temperature. Add eggs, one at a time, keeping mixer on the lowest speed in order to prevent too much air from destroying proper consistency of batter; mix just until each egg has been incorporated into batter. Fold in cranberries very gently with rubber spatula, being careful not to break them; pour filling into crust. Bake at 350 degrees F. for 40 minutes. If ingredients are not at room temperature, add 5 minutes baking time. Remove from oven and let stand on counter top for 10 minutes while you prepare the topping. (This is a very essential step.) Do not turn off oven heat.

Topping:
2 cups dairy sour cream
1/4 cup sugar
1/2 teaspoon mint extract

Combine sour cream, sugar, and mint extract with rubber spatula in plastic bowl. Spread evenly over top of baked filling. Return to 350 degree F. oven for 10 minutes. Remove from oven and place in refrigerator to cool immediately. Cover with piece of cardboard. Never cover with aluminum foil or plastic wrap; they will cause moisture to collect on topping of cake. Keep covered in refrigerator for 2 days to mellow. Remove from refrigerator several hours before serving. The center texture should be custardy.

Winnifred C. Jardine, a home economics consultant and former food editor for the Deseret News, *has authored* The No Gimmick Diet, Famous Mormon Recipes, Mormon Country Cooking, *and* Managing Your Meals. *The cranberry mint cheesecake recipe was taken from Myra Chanin,* Mother Wonderful's Cheesecakes and Other Goodies, *Bantam Books.*

HOLIDAY RECIPES

by Helen Thackeray

If you think Ruby Grapefruit sounds ordinary, believe me it is not. I never serve it without getting raves. The color says "holiday," and the tart-sweet flavor is a nice contrast to hearty holiday fare. It is a great beginning to a party meal. "Try it. You'll like it."

Ruby Grapefruit

4 large grapefruit
1 recipe Ruby Sauce

Peel and section grapefruit.* Chill.

To serve: Pour undiluted Ruby Sauce over grapefruit sections in serving bowl. Serve 5 sections plus sauce in each individual serving dish. Spoon some of the sauce over each. Makes 8 servings.

*To section grapefruit, first peel with a sharp knife (a serrated knife works well). Cut deep enough to remove white membrane underlayer. Then cut close to membrane on each side of fruit wedge and carefully slip out whole section. After the first wedge comes out (you may cut on one side only), work tip of knife under edge of section and roll it away from the membrane on the other side. This will keep the sections larger. Squeeze out juice from membrane over grape-fruit sections. Each grapefruit will yield 11 sections.

Ruby (Raspberry) Sauce

1 package (10 ounces) frozen raspberries
2 tablespoons sugar (omit where sauce is used with sweet fruit)

Heat raspberries and sugar in a small saucepan until berries are thawed and juice flows. Puree in blender or food mill. Strain to remove seeds. Chill. Makes about 1 cup.

What is Christmas without popcorn balls? Make them caramel corn and you have created a holiday masterpiece. This recipe makes the very best caramel corn I have ever eaten.

Caramel Corn

1 1/2 cups sugar
1 cup brown sugar
3/4 cup water
1/2 cup dark corn syrup
1 1/2 cups raw Spanish peanuts
1 teaspoon salt
1/4 cup margarine
1 teaspoon vanilla
1 teaspoon baking soda
4 quarts popped corn, warmed

Combine sugars, water, and corn syrup in a large heavy saucepan. Cook to 230 degrees F. on a candy thermometer. Add peanuts. Cook to 280 degrees F. Add salt and butter. Cook to 290 degrees F. Remove from heat. Add combined vanilla and soda.

Pour warm corn into a large pan, such as a dishpan. Pour syrup over corn and stir quickly to coat all the corn. Dump onto a slab and spread thin. When cool enough to handle, form into balls. Or let cool completely, then break into pieces. Stores well in plastic bags.

Altitude adjustments may need to be made. Recipe temperatures are for sea level. Adjust these temperatures at higher altitudes this way:

1. Hold your thermometer in a pan of boiling water for a few minutes. Record the temperature when the water boils. Water boils at a lower temperature at higher altitudes. For example, in many Salt Lake City locations, water boils at 203 degrees F.

2. Subtract the reading you have recorded from the boiling point of water at sea level. Example: 212 degrees F. minus 203 degrees F. = 9 degrees F.

3. Subtract this difference from the temperature given in the recipe. Example: 230 degrees F. minus 9 degrees F. = 221 degrees F.

290 degrees F. minus 9 degrees F. = 281 degrees F.

Try these party meatballs on a Christmas buffet table. They look festive, have a light texture and pleasing taste, and are easy to prepare.

Holiday Meatballs

1 pound lean ground beef
1 egg, slightly beaten
1/2 cup milk
1 small onion, chopped fine
1/8 teaspoon dried sage
1/2 teaspoon salt
1/8 teaspoon pepper
30 Ritz crackers, rolled into crumbs (a food processor works great)
2 tablespoons finely chopped fresh mint, or use 1 teaspoon crumbled dried mint

Combine ingredients and mix well. Form into balls about 1 inch in diameter. Place on baking sheet about 4-5 inches from the top unit of your oven. Broil until well browned, 5 to 8 minutes. Makes about 3 dozen meatballs.

Holiday Sauce

1/2 cup catsup
1 cup sweet and sour sauce (I use a 7-ounce jar of Dynasty brand sauce)
1/4 cup cider vinegar
1 1/2 teaspoons cornstarch
1/2 teaspoon salt
1/2 teaspoon ground ginger
1 can (8 ounces) chunk pineapple and juice
10 to 12 whole maraschino cherries, drained well

Combine all ingredients except pineapple and cherries. Cook and stir over medium heat until thickened. Add meatballs and fruit. Heat together a few minutes. Serve with cocktail picks from a chafing dish or hot casserole.

Carrot cake is a favorite. It tastes good; it keeps wells; it is made from commonly available, comparatively inexpensive ingredients. It is not as rich or heavy as fruitcake. And in this recipe, it is even less so. See if you don't agree that this is the best carrot cake you've ever tasted.

French Carrot Cake

   2 cups sugar
   4 large eggs
   1 cup salad oil
   2 cups all-purpose flour
   3 teaspoons cinnamon
   2 teaspoons baking soda
   1 teaspoon salt
   3 cups finely shredded or ground carrots
   2 teaspoons cider vinegar

Combine sugar, eggs, and oil in the large bowl of the electric mixer and beat well. Add and mix flour, cinnamon, soda, and salt. Mix in carrots and vinegar. Pour into a greased 9 x 13-inch baking pan. Bang the pan 3 times on the kitchen counter. Bake at 350 degrees F. for 40-45 minutes. When cool, spread with cream cheese frosting.

Cream Cheese Frosting

   1/4 pound margarine, melted
   1 package (3 ounces) cream cheese
   2 cups powdered sugar
   1/2 teaspoon vanilla
   1 cup chopped walnuts or pecans, if desired

Combine all ingredients except nuts. Mix until glossy. Spread over cooled cake. Top with chopped nuts.

Helen Thackeray was assistant equipment editor at Woman's Home Companion *magazine in New York, then rose through the ranks to manager of the General Foods Test Kitchens. She is the author of* Lion House Recipes *and coauthor of* The Mormon Family Cook Book.

BECAUSE OF ONE SMALL CHILD

By Mabel Jones Gabbott

Let me tell you about a child, whose birth
Was breathed on the wind-lift of an angels' chorus;
In the meridian of time this hope of earth
Was born to Mary—a God, committed for us.

Let me tell you how heaven rejoiced, starred
With light to the vast reaches of galactic space;
How humble ones brought bleating gifts; from far,
Far miles star-seekers came to see his face.

And let it be witnessed that the hope remains
Of race and creeds and color reconciled
In peace after the wise Magian way,
Of hate imprisoned, selfishness in chains,
Of brotherhood, because of one small child,
Cradled in a manger in the hay.

FOR ALL MANKIND

by Mabel Jones Gabbott

Of Time

Into the midst of time, between the old
Law and the new, he came as was foretold.

Yet, all of time is his; his are the sun
And starshine. All the measured hours that run

Between are in his time . . . and so are we,
And they who were the very first to see

A sunset on the earth, or hear the birds
Carol his praises; they who heard his words,

And all who follow after to time's rim
Before and since the blessed Christmas morn
Are rich with time and life because of him.
For unto all mankind, the Son was born.

Of Place

That was an ancient year, a distant land
When Magi, richly dressed with gifts in hand.

Had traced the starlight unto Bethlehem,
Had seen the Holy Child, and worshipped him,

Yet all of earth is his, the restless dune,
The steadfast mountains, and the sea and moon,

The crowded city, trimmed and tinseled bright,
The country roadway drenched in lunar light.

Though stars are quiet now above the place
Where Christ was born, his light will always fill
With penetrating rays the ends of space,
As surely as it crowned Judea's hill.

SURPRISE ME FOR CHRISTMAS

by Shirley Sealy

"It's almost morning, Shirl. What you haven't finished doesn't matter. Go to bed," was my husband's annual statement as he woke up from where he'd fallen asleep putting toys together or waiting to eat the cookies the children had left for Santa. "Shirl, you're killing yourself. You need to get some sleep."

But for me Christmas was surprises, set like a scene on the stage, with every detail finished. I had to see that vision of shimmering beauty all put together before I could go to bed, and Santa could never come until every child was asleep.

This was often a source of controversy with my husband and me. He came from a family of six and I from a family of eight. We were both number three in line. We grew up around the corner from each other, went to the same school from junior high on, and had the same religion, goals, and values. But our ideas about Christmas morning and Christmas Eve were different.

His family opened all the presents from other people on Christmas Eve and only Santa's presents in the morn-

ing. In my family we saved all the packages until morning. Surprise was the name of Christmas for me. One year when I disobeyed the rules, I learned how important that was.

I grew up in Idaho where Christmas was always associated with snow—snow that blew, drifted, and crusted. More than once our back porch was snowed in so we couldn't get out of the door. But on the immediate other side of the porch drift, the ground was bare and frozen. I played on drifts that were so hard I could walk on the top, yet so deep that if I fell through I couldn't get out of the hole by myself.

We lived during the Depression and had few luxuries, even for Christmas. But my mother was a skilled seamstress and my father a talented finish carpenter and jack-of-all-trades. Our Christmas presents were homemade or items we had needed for a long time but that were saved while we sacrificed a little longer. Always we were surprised and delighted at Christmas.

Mother was quiet, truthful, and made us all feel loved and wanted. My father was even-tempered but full of tricks and tall tales. There was no swearing in our home. Mother was a cultured woman, though she had very little education, and she always used excellent grammar. My father was energetic, talented, a good actor, and full of surprises.

I remember cold Christmas mornings when we children stood freezing in our nightshirts in the kitchen while Father slipped into the front room where the tree stood. He'd report: "Santa's been here, and oh, my goodness, what is that? Why I didn't believe he would ever bring such a thing. There's one here for . . ."

Then he would name each of us while he lit the fire in the big potbellied stove and the candles on the Christmas tree. Then he'd call us in. No matter how thrilled or surprised we were, my father played his part on a higher pitch than we did as children.

Christmas Eve was a time for decorating the tree and making homemade wrapping for the presents we gave each other and put on the tree. But Christmas morning we each had at least one gift, and it was a surprise. There was always an orange in the toe of our stocking. Oranges were hard to find and afford during the winter.

Mother was a stalwart, and she always managed to make us each a present we didn't expect. She filled our lives with warmth, courage, and strength. Looking back, I realize it was Mother's love, sacrifice, and trust that was really the spirit of year-round Christmas in our home.

One Christmas I learned those principles the hard way. And I learned what it really meant to be surprised on Christmas morning.

The closest shopping stores were nineteen miles away in Burley and Rupert. Sears & Roebuck, Wards, and J.C. Penney were the big stores in those days. At Christmastime Mother and Father always made a trip to Burley or Rupert a few days before the holiday. Nineteen miles was quite a distance to go in the cars we drove back then. I knew that a trip just before Christmas meant they would buy whatever they were going to give us and then hide it until the big day.

That Christmas I needed shoes. I'd been wearing cardboard in the bottom of my only pair for quite a while. I had seen a pair of black suede slippers. (We called shoes "slippers" if they had a strap and a button across the foot or around the ankle. Anything else was an oxford, with shoelaces. I had picked out a pair of slippers in the catalog.) The shoes were the only thing on my Christmas list.

The day after my parents went to Burley, I got home from school before the others and was there alone. I had a feeling Mother would get me the slippers, but I wanted to know for sure. I couldn't wait.

There weren't many places to hide gifts in a three-room home with no basement, two beds in every room, and bottled fruit under the beds. One pre-Christmas rule in our family was that we didn't hunt for or peek into any packages we might accidentally find. We were on the honor system. I knew it was wrong to search, but I searched anyway.

The only suitcase we had was on a shelf above the closet. The closet was a board on the wall in the corner of the bedroom. There was a curtain around it. On the wall next to the closet was a dresser. The suitcase seemed to be a very good hiding place.

I climbed up on the dresser and reached inside the suitcase. I could barely reach by standing on my tiptoes, and I almost made the whole thing fall down on top of me. But there in the corner was a package. And inside the package were the shoes I had asked for. I tried them on, and they fit. They were beautiful. I was so thrilled I wanted to yell. Finally I slipped the shoes back in place and waited for Christmas, which was four days away.

I will never forget those four days. I carried a secret I couldn't share with anyone. I would rather have died than let Mother know I had broken her trust in me. So I had to keep silent and wait. It wasn't fun, nothing like I'd thought it would be, to know that secret. In fact, I was miserable. I wanted to share my good news but had to remain silent and alone with my good fortune.

I will never forget how hard it was on Christmas morning to act genuinely surprised and excited about my gift. The thrill of that Christmas was gone, eaten up by my decision to break the rule. I guess I was a pretty good actress, because Mother never guessed I had been deceitful.

That year I learned that surprises, gifts, and secrets are only fun when they can be shared with others. It is a lesson that has stayed with me through the years and has helped me rear my children. I shared Mother's lecture about the honor system with them, and it became a rule. Often I told our children exactly where their surprises would be kept.

"This closet has been cleaned out for Christmas gifts. Don't look inside any packages in this closet or you will spoil your Christmas. Of course, if you don't want to be surprised, just go ahead," I would tell them.

Letting them know the hiding place took away the challenge of the search. My children tell me now that they never thought of looking at a present before Christmas, and they've carried this tradition into their own families.

As for me, I still love Christmas. My husband surprises me with something just for me and fills my stocking with surprise packages to unwrap on Christmas morning. Of course, all the while he's telling me how nice it was to open gifts on Christmas Eve.

Shirley Sealy has written fifteen books—thirteen novels and two works of nonfiction: Forever After *and* The Beginning of Forever.

THE CHRISTMAS WHEN THE WIND DID NOT BLOW

by Jaroldeen Edwards

I was raised on the prairies of southern Alberta where the wind always blows. In the springtime the wind is a trumpet waking the sleeping things of the earth.

In the summer the wind is warm and dry and carries with it the smell of ripening wheat fields and distant mountaintops.

The autumn wind is filled with gold, the fine sprinkle of dried leaves turned to fairy dust and thrown upon a riotous world. Then December comes and the first gentle, wind-blown snow blankets the earth.

Our family loved the wind. It was as much a part of our daily experience as the breath we drew. Of course, in the winter the wind could literally take our breath away. Sometimes we would step out the front door, dressed to the teeth in ski pants, parka, fur-lined boots, mittens, and heavy scarves that covered everything but our eyes, and the wind would hit us as we ran to the school bus. That wind could cut through the thickest thermal underwear, the fuzziest down, all the warmest protection man could devise. We loved it anyway.

As Christmastime approached the snow would blow deep, stacked on either side of the streets, sometimes almost shoulder high. At recess we played fox and geese, tramping big wheels in the snow with our boots and running and chasing each other along the narrow paths we had stamped.

On the days when Mother said we could catch the late bus after school, we would play for half an hour in the Duff Addition, the playing field next to the school. There were no trees or plantings to speak of. It didn't look like much of a park. But it was a wonderful place to play.

In the winter, filled with snow, the Duff Addition was like a great blank page on which we could write our own games and create our own delights. We made snow angels, swooping our arms and legs to make wings and skirts around the impressions of our bodies. The trick was to get back up without making footprints or handprints on our "angel."

We made snow fortresses and had snowball fights. We rode Eagle Flyer sleds down every incline. And always

129

the wind was our companion, snatching at our scarves, catching up our snowballs, coating our lashes with crystals of snow, and, finally, sending us home when the persistent chill would at last penetrate even to the marrow of young and hardy bones.

Mother was stake MIA president, and father was the bishop. The stake was putting on a three-act Christmas play and a holiday dance, and Mother was trying to coordinate the planning and decorating committees for both events. Often we would burst in the door after school to find her immersed in a meeting with three or four of her board members. She was also involved in the PTA and helped organize the school Christmas concert.

All six of us children were involved in our own Christmas events—parties, the Primary Pageant, MIA service projects, choirs, piano recitals, as well as all the usual plannings that surround the Christmas season. The hum of expectations was like the urgency of the constant prairie wind.

Father was busy, too. Tramping in and out of the house in his huge buffalo fur coat. His white Stetson, molded and shaped by wear until it seemed a biological part of his profile, gave him the look of a dapper Wild Bill Hickok. They were shipping cattle at the stockyards, and the work was hard for him to oversee in the snow. It was also time for tithing settlement. Several new families had recently moved into the ward from Australia and Britain—families who had endured World War II and its

aftermath and who were beginning again. These were families who needed a great deal of shepherding, and Father knew a lot about caring for people as well as for animals. He knew a lot about caring, period.

Sometimes we came home to an empty house with notes pinned everywhere. "Do your homework. I will be home at 5:30. Please put casserole in oven. Was at your school today. Heard choir. Sounded wonderful. Can't wait. Love you. Mother." Or, "Emergency! Had to go to play rehearsal. Put away clean clothes on bed. Home soon. Mother."

The house was beginning to fill up with rolls of wrapping paper and boxes of Christmas decorations. We were prancing with eagerness to put up the tree. Father unexpectedly brought it home one night. He had been visiting a ranch, checking on a herd, and the owner had given him a tree replete with real pinecones and an abandoned bird's nest tucked within the upper branches. The wind was blowing that night with a sharp vigor that promised harsh weather.

A blizzard struck that night, and the next day we had to dig our way out of the house and the driveway because there was so much to be done. But we were like the wind. Nothing could stop us.

The pre-Christmas days whirled by. The three-act play was finished, and the Christmas school concert was a success. The holiday dance went off without a hitch. It was time now for the "relative" parties. First my mother's family came: all ten of her brothers and sisters with husbands, wives, and children. They filled our home to overflowing, and we giggled in the playroom downstairs as we donned sheets, tinsel, bathrobes, and towels to put on the traditional Christmas pageant.

Some of us joked about what we were doing. It was our way of telling our cousins we were too old for such things, but what could we do? Our parents still expected it. The truth was, we loved the Christmas pageant, and still wished we could be Mary, or Joseph, and hold the tiny child.

Then came the evening for my father's family—a formal dinner for just Grandma and Grandpa, dignified and quiet. We felt a little careful in their presence because we so wanted them to approve of us. I can't believe we actually dared ask them to play charades that year. They, who never played games. I will never forget Grandfather singling me out to help him with his part. His white moustache and wonderful, clear blue eyes. His handsome face smiling. He put his arm around my shoulder and stood pointing far into the distance as though showing me the way. His pointing finger traced an imaginary path in the air and my father called out immediately—"There's a Long Long Trail A-Winding!" Grandfather looked as pleased as if he had won a gold medal.

It was all a whirl. The parties, the decorations, friends and relatives. Into the car, out of the car, on the phone, at the church, to and from school, not to mention the everyday chores—and all the usual cleaning, laundry, dinners to fix, homework to do. We raced and spilled into Christmas Eve, spinning in the great tumble of a big Mormon family preparing for the greatest event of the year.

Christmas Eve morning dawned crisp and cold. Downstairs Mother and Father were standing in the kitchen, and Daddy was wearing his buffalo coat.

"I need to go out to take the boxes to the widows," he said, "then I'll be home to finish up in the basement."

For the past three weeks it seemed that Father had spent every spare moment in the workroom in the basement, which had been declared off-limits. We all knew he was creating a family gift in his workshop.

"That's fine," Mother said. "I'm going to start on the baking."

"Baking!" I wailed. "It's Christmas Eve day! What are you going to be baking?"

"With all my responsibilities this year," Mother said, "I haven't had time to do any of my Christmas baking. No fruitcakes. No Christmas pudding. No candy. People will be dropping in all through the holidays. I have to have something on hand. Listen, dear, why don't you go skating?" I knew she was trying to get me out of the kitchen so she could get to work.

The boys were all too busy doing last-minute things to go skating with me, and my little sister took one look out the window at the wind blowing the drifts against the hedge and said, "Too cold."

The older boys went off to visit friends and drop off last-minute presents. My brother Malcolm and I sat idly in the breakfast room. Several times we asked Mother if we could help, but she waved us off. "No. Just go have a good time. It's your first day free from school. Have fun." She did not mention how we were supposed to accomplish that.

Right after supper the phone rang. It was Muriel Gentleman's mother. Muriel was a girl in my class. Her father was a business associate of my father's. The family had moved to Lethbridge the previous year from northern Scotland. They were quiet, intelligent people with a distinctive accent that made their conversation sound as though it was read from Shakespeare.

With the typical insularity of youth I admired Muriel, but it had never occurred to me that she was an "ordinary" girl who would like to do the plain old ordinary and crazy things my friends and I did. So I kept a neat pattern—I was Muriel's friend, but I never dreamed of including her in my "other" circle of friends. Besides, my other friends were members of the Church, and Muriel was not a Mormon.

The Gentlemans always seemed to be happy. Mrs. Gentleman, a plump, pretty woman with brown hair pulled back into a neat bun and a gentle halo of natural curls framing her face, was always dressed formally in a dark neat

dress with a white lace collar, pearls, hose, and pumps. Their father was a handsome man, given to tweeds, with a perennial pipe in his mouth. We thought the pipe a real touch of worldly sophistication, but vaguely scandalous because it was such abiding evidence that they did not live the Word of Wisdom. It never dawned on us to think that such self-reliant people might be lonely.

Our relationship with the Gentlemans was one of courteous regard and distance. It came as a shock to me, therefore, when I heard my mother say, "Yes, Jaroldeen and Malcolm would be happy to come. Thank you for inviting them, Helen."

The Gentlemans were having a small gathering for their children's friends. Very informal. And they had invited my brother and me to come over.

"It's Christmas Eve!" I protested. "I don't want to go anywhere on Christmas Eve. Least of all the Gentlemans'. I hardly know them."

"It would be rude of you not to go," Mother said firmly. "Muriel is a friend of yours, and this is their first Christmas in Canada. You only need to stay a short time. Father will drive you over and come to get you."

Mother didn't fool me. I knew she wanted to get me out of the house. I'd been driving her crazy with my pointless wandering all afternoon. So Father bundled us into the car, and we drove over to the Gentlemans' home. Father's car drove off and we walked through the gate and up the path to the wide porch. The front door opened. Yellow light spilled out onto the snow, and Mr. and Mrs. Gentleman waved us up the path.

"How dear of you to come!" Mrs. Gentleman's gentle, accented voice was filled with welcome. "You are such lovely children to spare us a part of your precious Christmas Eve."

Muriel came happily out of the living room, her eyes shining. Her sister and brother flanked her. There were three other friends in the room. That was all. The house was quiet and smelled of apples and cinnamon. Everyone was dressed in lovely but simple clothes, and a huge fire crackled in the living room.

The house was only partially furnished, with a few scattered rugs on the shining hardwood floors. The Gentlemans had lost a great deal in the war, but their living room was graced with a grand piano and a large rocking chair on each side of the fireplace. Mr. and Mrs. Gentleman took their places in the rocking chairs, and the rest of us sat somewhat awkwardly on a couch and the floor.

Everything in the house was spotless and there was a wonderful sense of peace and quiet. There were refreshments on a tray in the kitchen, and Muriel and Mrs. Gentleman served them as though they were serving nectar and ambrosia. The refreshments were spiced cider and Scottish shortbread. Nothing else. But it was served in crystal cups, with crisply laundered napkins. Muriel's face beamed.

"I love these shortbreads!" she exclaimed. "Mother only makes this recipe at Christmastime. We wait all year for it." The family laughed gently, warmly, and we found ourselves leaning back and laughing, too. It was a comfortable feeling.

There were moments of silence in the room, but they were strangely sweet, as though silence was nothing to fear. Then Mrs. Gentleman turned to us and said, "Now, I know you are all gifted and wonderful. Muriel has told us. We would love it if you would share those gifts with us on this special night." Her voice was gentle and slow. She was an unhurried woman.

Mrs. Gentleman had really done her homework, because she knew everything about us. We were all preparing for the Arts Competition in February. Some of us were playing piano, some were going to sing, and some were preparing dramatic readings. The Arts Competition was the scariest thing about growing up in Alberta. Once a year your mother and teachers made you do it—and it was awful. You stood in front of these judges in this great big auditorium and made a fool of yourself—at least that's what I always felt I did. But I entered everything anyway and then just died because I had to go through with it.

We were reluctant to perform, but somehow Mrs. Gentleman made it seem quite natural. She turned to Mr. Gentleman and said, "Father, I have always thought that performing among a group of friends is one of the best ways to prepare for a competition. Don't you agree?" and Mr. Gentleman nodded sagaciously.

Well, somehow she convinced us, and we didn't feel silly or awkward. We felt as though what we were doing was somehow important, and appreciated. One by one we performed, and everyone in the room listened with absolute attention. We enjoyed each other and began to think we were truly gifted. After each performance Mrs. Gentleman would say something—a very specific compliment—to make each performer feel they had done something unique and extraordinary.

After I finished playing the piano she looked at me and said, with her soft Scottish burr, "Jar-r-roldeen, I have never heard such accurate timing. You must have an internal metronome. Even your ritards were done in perfect proportion."

And I, who thought myself wonderfully cynical and above the need to be complimented, felt myself glowing in a sense of increased worth, as though her words had helped me find something worthwhile in myself.

Their tree was a simple affair, with white, cut paper ornaments they had made themselves. They looked like delicate three-dimensional snowflakes. And white ribbons tied in little bows. It was

the first time I had seen ribbons on a tree.

After one hour Mr. Gentleman spoke. "Now children, it is time we return you to your own hearths. But first, may we read a word of Christmas beauty with you?" He pulled down a huge old Bible, and in the hushed light of that clean, bare room he read a few hallowed words of Christmas scripture.

I was suddenly struck with the universality of the Christmas message. Non-Mormons and Mormons alike treasured it. "Thank you for sharing some of your Christmas Eve with us," he said as he closed the book. "We'll not bother your parents. If you don't mind riding in the back of my pickup, I'll drive you home."

All of the Gentlemans came. Laughing in their joyful way, they brought blankets and lined the bed of the truck. "Now you must keep down!" Mrs. Gentleman fussed. We all snuggled down against the sides of the truck bed, and Mr. and Mrs. Gentleman got in the cab.

It was a fifteen-minute drive to our house, and we were to be dropped off first. We lived in a park area on the very outskirts of town. Across from our home there was nothing but trees and the lake. There were no street lights where we lived. As we drove down the avenue out of town we began to sing carols. At first we shouted jovially "Deck the Halls" and "Jingle Bells," but as we drove by the lake we began to sing "It Came upon the Midnight Clear." Mr. Gentleman heard our

voices, stopped the motor, and rolled down the window so he could hear the rest of the hymn.

We sang the last words of the carol, and we sat in the wondrously clear night and felt the spirit of Christmas reach down and settle over us as surely as the quiet snow covers the waiting earth.

"Malcolm," I whispered to my brother. "Listen."

He was as filled with the beauty of the moment as I, and he turned to me with a puzzled look.

"The wind," I explained. "Listen. The wind has stopped blowing."

We looked in wonder. Not the tiniest flake was disturbed. Our hair lay smooth and the stars' light shone down through silent air that did not move. Almost together we sighed with a deep sense of peace in that silent night of silver and blue.

Mr. Gentleman restarted the motor and drove us down the lane to our home. We thanked them for the evening and walked silently up the front walk.

In contrast to what we'd just experienced, our house was full of Christmas confusion. The older boys were home and had brought friends with them. The hammering was still going on in the basement. Every light in the house blazed. Carols were playing on the record player, and the younger children were arguing over who had used the last of the tape. Mother was putting the last pudding in the steamer and looking at the kitchen in despair.

135

Malcolm and I stood in the doorway and our faces must have said a lot. "What time is it?" Mother asked, surprised to see us.

"Almost nine o'clock," Malcolm said. "We'll help you, and then I guess we'll go to bed."

Something in his voice made her stop and look into his eyes. Without a word she reached behind her and took off her apron. "No," she said. "I'll leave this." She put aside the half-finished pudding and walked to the basement door. "Charles," she called down the stairs to my father, "could you come here for a moment, please?" He came up the stairs and they talked quietly, and then Father walked to the front hall.

"In the living room, everyone," he called, and the family came from every corner of the house. The visiting teenagers left for their own homes, and Father and Mother gathered us into the beautiful front room. The tree was lighted and hung with the bounty of ornaments gathered in years of marriage. Father lit the logs in the fireplace, and Mother sat in her armchair and smiled at us. Her eyes were weary but filled with love.

"Did I ever tell you about my first Christmas in Canada?" she asked. "We had come from comfortable living in Utah to a barren homestead in the prairie wilderness." She told how her mother had made them a Christmas tree from pieces of broom handle because there were no trees on the prairie.

Father talked to us about the Savior's mission. "What think ye of Christ?" he said. Then he bore his testimony of His divine mission.

With a smile Mother passed around her fudge, which had not set properly. We loved it, even though it stuck to our fingers. "Never do things in haste," she sighed, looking at the gooey plate, but we laughed and told her it was the best we'd ever tasted.

Daddy turned off all the lights but those on the tree, and we sang "Silent Night." While we were singing we heard the shutters shake outside, and a blast of wind hit the house.

Father went to the front door and looked out. A great wind was rolling across the land, it was full of snow and motion and excitement. It would bring needed moisture and liven the earth wherever it touched. The wind would fill our nostrils and challenge us to be strong. It would make our lives richer, more exciting, fuller than any mere life of calm and comfort.

We listened to its exuberant rush, and thought how wonderful it would be to wake up in the morning to the new snow.

"Oh, Mother," I said. "I love the wind. I wouldn't ever want to live without it, but once in a while it's important that it stops blowing long enough for us to rest and to listen."

Mother bent and kissed me. "I know," she said.

And she did know. She had understood.

I guess all those years ago I learned

the lesson of Christmas from two women. From Mrs. Gentleman, who had learned to savor the calm; but also from my mother, who lived her life in a whirlwind, but who also had the wisdom and the will to know when to gather her family in silence to hear the quiet message of stillness and peace.

*Jaroldeen Edwards is the author of several novels released nationally—*A Woman Between *and* The Mountains of Eden *among them—and one published by Deseret Book,* The Chaldean Star.

PRICELESS GIFTS

by Daryl V. Hoole

Once, several years ago, I played an unusual and unexpected role in someone else's Christmas. Much to my surprise, I was a Christmas present.

Actually, my part in this story is quite insignificant—almost anyone, depending on the circumstances, could serve as a Christmas gift. I share the experience because the principle involved could make almost anyone's Christmas observance meaningful and unique.

Two cousins invited my husband, Hank, and me to their home for dinner one evening just after Christmas. They explained that another couple, Ron and Renee, would be joining us. Apparently Renee had read some of my writings and had subsequently expressed an interest in meeting me, just as many readers are interested in meeting authors of books they enjoy and find useful. I sensed there might be more to the situation, but it wasn't until the story unfolded over dinner that night that I fully understood and appreciated what had taken place.

Ron, a construction contractor, had lost his business. His current job, working as a high school custodian, barely

provided the essentials for his growing family. With Christmas approaching, there wasn't much money to spend on gifts, so Ron and Renee agreed to give each other things that cost little—or even nothing. In fact, they made a contest of it to see who could spend the least on otherwise meaningful gifts.

They told us that Renee had purchased only buttons for several shirts she made her husband. (Materials on hand, such as fabric, didn't count.) She had also asked talented friends to record some of Ron's favorite music in exchange for babysitting. And she promised to bake him a pie each month during the coming year.

Despite the simplicity and prudence of these gifts, Ron's presents to his wife cost even less—nothing. He gave her a series of sewing lessons, for which he'd traded the sewing teacher a roof repair, and piano lessons that he exchanged for his carpet-cleaning services. He made Renee a bird feeder (to involve the children) and a bread box out of odds and ends around the house. And he spent hours writing their family's history, which he presented to her as another gift.

When Ron learned that some friends were related to me, he had an idea for another gift: giving Renee the chance to talk with me, one-on-one, about some of my ideas. It would be a fun and unusual Christmas present. My cousins agreed to not only arrange the meeting but also to host a dinner party. Ron accepted their hospitality, offering to return the favor by holding a dinner at his home and inviting friends he knew my cousins would like to meet. So, in effect, a number of people became gifts that Christmas.

The night of our dinner party, Ron showed us the certificate he had given Renee on Christmas to announce the occasion. As we talked about the holiday season just past, Ron and Renee enthusiastically declared they had never had a more meaningful or enjoyable Christmas. Their gifts may have cost less, but because they were gifts born of the heart, in many ways they were priceless.

Daryl V. Hoole is the author of A House of Order, The Art of Homemaking, The Art of Teaching Children, The Joys of Homemaking, The Season to Prepare, *and* Our Own Society.

WARM HANDS FOR CHRISTMAS

by Marilynne Todd Linford

"Oh, it's cold out there! Not much snow this year, but the cold penetrates these old bones," Grandma said as she took off her wraps.

"Well, sit here for a few minutes," Mama suggested. "David just put enough coal in the Majestic for a few more hours."

I was in the next room sitting with my back against the wall where the heat from the stove penetrated. It was the second warmest place in the house. Grandma had the first. I had been working down in Uncle Frank's stable all morning with a wheelbarrow and pitchfork, and I was tired and cold. I had a blanket around my head and shoulders kind of like a tent to keep the heat in. When Papa saw I had finished in the stable, he told me I could read until lunch. I liked to sit here and read and listen. Sometimes I did more listening than reading when Mama and Grandma got talking. Sometimes it got very interesting.

"Ruthie, it's a shame you and David have to live like this." Grandma started in on a subject I had heard many times. "Frank and Ruby have a tree decorated.

Ruby is making gingerbread. Here you sit, my beautiful daughter, scrubbing potatoes and wondering where your next penny will come from."

"I'm not complaining, Mother. We have this home."

"Yes, and it's so big we can only pay the interest on the mortgage each month. Oh, it's so cold," Grandma added.

"Spring will come, and then summer, and we'll all be complaining about the heat. Anyway, you know how hard David tries to find work. It is not his fault there is a depression and they don't teach penmanship in the high schools any more. Only four men in the neighborhood have regular jobs. And think of Kenneth and June and Edna. The Lord has blessed me. I'll not complain."

"Well, it breaks my heart to have Christmas just two days away. There is no tree, no gifts, no fancy Christmas dinner. Why, at Frank's . . . "

"Mother, I know Frank has so much more. Would you rather go there for Christmas?"

"No, no. It's here with you I want to

140

stay. You are the sweetest, most gentle daughter. But, such a dreary Christmas. It's almost more than I can stand," concluded Grandma.

"It's just Kenneth I'm concerned about." (My half-reading, half-listening suddenly became 100 percent listening as Mama said my name.) "We do have the aprons we made for June and Edna. Your embroidery on them is lovely, Mother. But you can't give an apron to a fourteen-year-old boy."

"Grandma, come see our slide. Papa made us a slide!" That was Edna's voice, my seven-year-old sister. She was good at interrupting many things.

"I will, Eddy, in a few minutes, dear. First I have a surprise for your mother."

"A sweet from Aunt Ruby?"

"No, Eddy, not this time. This is something for your mama and papa and me. Run along and I'll look out the back window at your slide."

"Here, Ruthie," Grandma said. "Frank sent you Tuesday's *Deseret News*. He thought you would enjoy catching up on what's happening in the world."

"Frank is so extravagant. That newspaper cost ten cents," said Mama in her "well-he-did-it-again" voice.

"I know. But since we have it, let's enjoy it."

"You read to me while I set the table," Mama agreed.

"I wished they'd get back to the subject of my Christmas," I thought. I knew we were poor, but I didn't think we were so poor that they were think-

ing of giving me an apron.

Grandma began. "The Daily Thought is from Benjamin Franklin. 'He that hath a trade hath an estate.' Maybe, Ruthie, it's Benjamin Franklin's fault that David can't find work."

"Mother, how could that be?"

"Well, if he hadn't been such a printer—maybe if the typewriter and printing machines hadn't been so improved—David would still be teaching at East High."

"Mother, Mother."

"Oh, I know. But when the school district has diplomas printed instead of engrossed, what's this world coming to? Frank's trade hasn't made him an estate, not in the least."

"What else is in the news?" Mother asked to keep Grandma off the subject of Papa and his penmanship. Papa was one of the best penmen in America. He engrossed names on things for the University of Utah and the Church and lots of businesses. I liked to watch him at his lettering desk gracefully moving the pen across the pages, blotting, dipping his pen in the ink, wiping it with care, and then making big and small strokes with his hand again. Once, when he had time, Papa wrote my name in all different sizes and kinds of writing. I saved it in my drawer.

"Well, the weather will be unsettled and slightly warmer tonight. The maximum temperature will be 29." Grandma's voice came to my ear again. "And the barber code is declared illegal because of the Utah law against monopolies. Who can afford a haircut, anyway?" Grandma asked, not expecting an answer. "Here's something interesting," she said, turning a page. "Henry Ford says that money is the greatest mystery of all. He advises young America to learn and keep working . . . Ruthie! . . . He says that business is all right and improving daily. He says, quote, 'There is no depression, now.' He should come to Salt Lake. . . . He was asked if he is 'bitterly opposed to liquor.' Listen to his answer. 'No, I wouldn't say that I am. We can't have men in our factory drinking on the job at all, though. We have fine, delicate machinery and a drinking man can't come in and operate it.' "

"He sounds like a good man," Mama responded.

"It says that holiday business is reported the best in years in Chicago. It may even exceed 1929," read Grandma. "Our business isn't better than anything," she said sharply. "Remember the Christmas of '29? David was teaching and had more business engrossing certificates than he could handle. That year the girls got dolls and barrettes and jacks. Kenneth got the nickel-plated BB gun. Those were the days."

"Yes," Mother said. "But this is 1933. I think . . . "

"Ruthie! Listen to this. Some students and clubs are renovating toys, it says, to make sure Santa visits every Salt Lake City home. Well, he won't come here. I know that. How can they say Santa will visit every child? Oh, my dear Kenneth. What can we do for him. He is such a good boy. He's too old for Santa. But a fourteen-year-old boy should have some Christmas."

"That's right!" I almost said out loud.

"Grandma! Did you look at me sliding?" Here was Edna again. Interrupting, again.

"Oh, Eddy, sweet, sweet Eddy. You are frozen. Here, sit by the stove and I'll go look out the window at that slide."

"Mama, what are we having for lunch?" Edna asked.

"Boiled potatoes, dear."

"Eddy, that slide looks very slippery. You be careful out there. You are Grandma's precious dark-haired beauty, you know." Grandma always talked that way to Edna. She loved to comb her hair at breakfast, and she ironed her clothes every time she wore them.

"Lunch is ready, Edna," said Mama. "Will you go get June and Papa and Kenneth."

"Yes, Mama. Where is Kenneth?"

"Oh, probably with Papa in the chicken coop," answered Mama.

I quickly put my coat back on and slipped out the front door so they wouldn't know I'd been listening.

Soon we were all sitting around the table. "A bowl of potatoes and a plate of raw turnips again," I inwardly complained.

"June, will you ask a blessing on the food to thank our Father for it?"

"Yes, Papa. Dear Father in Heaven. We are thankful that we have food to eat. Please help us to have enough money. Help Papa get jobs. Help us to have a nice Christmas. In the name of

Jesus Christ, Amen."

"Grandma, do you have any money?" Papa's voice interrupted the sound of turnips being chewed.

"No, David, I don't."

"Ruth, do you have any money?" he asked Mama.

"I don't. Do we need something?"

"Well, I have been thinking. This is the last day the stores will be open before Christmas. I have two quarters. . . ." Papa had a little tease in his voice. My heart, ears, and hopes listened. "Well, with that fifty cents," he continued, "I thought maybe Kenneth would like to walk up to J.C. Penney's with me to buy some gloves for his Christmas."

"Oh, Papa! Thank you. My hands do get cold," I said through the potatoes.

"Right after lunch we'll go," he said.

"Have you ever measured how far it is to Penney's?" Papa asked as we began our trek uphill.

"Well, it's five-and-a-half blocks to Grand Central," I said, figuring it out in my mind. "So, it would be nine blocks to Penney's. Is that a mile?"

"I think," Papa said, wrapping his scarf up over his chin, "that seven blocks equal a mile."

"Will we ever have a car, Papa?" I asked.

"I don't know, Kenneth, if I'll ever have one. But I know you will someday."

"Uncle Frank has had two cars," I said.

"Frank has many things," he an-swered as he put his scarf up over his nose and mouth. I knew I had said too much.

"Well, here we are at Grand Central," I said, trying to make conversation again.

My nose and ears were burning with cold. My hands were cold but not as bad as my head because I kept my hands deep in my coat pockets. I always had a secret fear, though, that I would slip on some ice with my hands in my pockets and not be able to get my hands out fast enough to catch myself. "When we're on our way home, I'll put my hands over my ears. The gloves will keep both my hands and ears warm that way," I thought.

We walked on past the Mexican restaurant whose name I couldn't pronounce. Past the bank. Past the church. Finally I could see Penney's.

"Well, we made it," I said, hoping Papa would forget the comment about Uncle Frank. Papa held the door for me, and I entered a new world. People laughing, talking, and buying. Cash registers ringing. Coins dropping in tills. The cold of the outside forgotten in the warmth of Penney's. I wondered if any of my friends would see me shopping with my Papa in Penney's. I felt Christmassy for the first time. I could smell roasted nuts, and I wished Mama were with us.

Papa's voice interrupted my trance. "Kenneth, the gloves are over here."

I could feel Papa's uncomfortable feeling. J.C. Penney's was like a foreign country to us. I wanted to stay and look and get really warm, maybe do some wishing. But I could tell Papa wanted to get done what we came for and get back home.

We went directly to where the gloves were stacked. I boldly picked up a pair and slipped my hand in. Papa looked at the price tag. Seventy-five cents. I picked up another pair. These were leather. Oh, how I'd love a leather pair! Papa looked at the price tag. Three dollars. I quickly took them off. I looked for what I thought would be the cheapest pair. I looked at the price tag. Sixty-five cents.

"Well," said Papa, "these are men's gloves. Let's try the boys' department. Your hands aren't too big yet."

There were two kinds for boys. They looked small. I tried a pair of knitted ones. My fingers were big and long. There was no price tag on them. "These will be good enough," said Papa.

We took them to the lady at the cash register to pay for them. She pushed some buttons and said, "That will be sixty cents."

"Sixty?" Papa and I gasped together.

The winter sun tried to warm our fronts as we walked back down the hill. But the signs of Christmas were too evident and too much a reminder of the bleakness of the sky and of our poverty.

As we retraced our steps the long nine blocks back home, I felt Papa's despair. Somehow I wasn't sad for me, but sad, a deep down sad, for Papa.

Soon we were back on Third East. I could see the school. We passed Uncle Frank's. And there was our house.

The crunch of the snow under our steps had become deafening. We walked to the back door. Papa held it for me.

I looked up into his eyes and saw not despair but faith as he put his hand on my shoulder and said simply, "There will be other Christmases."

And there were. As the years have passed and brought with them prosperity and maturity, never once have I put my hand in my pocket and felt dollars' worth of change that I haven't remembered how desperately I wanted just one dime to give my father that Christmas of '33.

Marilynne Linford is the author of Is Anyone Out There Building Mother's Self-Esteem? *and the coauthor of* I Hope They Call Me On a Mission Too!